Supporting musical development in the early years

Supporting early learning

Series Editors: Vicky Hurst and Jenefer Joseph

The focus of this series is on improving the effectiveness of early education. Policy developments come and go, and difficult decisions are often forced on those with responsibility for young children's well-being. This series aims to help with these decisions by showing how developmental approaches to early education provide a sound and positive basis for learning.

Each book recognizes that children from birth to 6 have particular developmental needs. This applies just as much to the acquisition of subject knowledge, skills and understanding as to other educational goals such as social skills, attitudes and dispositions. The importance of providing a learning environment which is carefully planned to stimulate children's own active learning is also stressed.

Throughout the series, readers are encouraged to reflect on the education being offered to young children, through revisiting developmental principles and using them to analyse their observations of children. In this way, readers can evaluate ideas about the most effective ways of educating young children and develop strategies for approaching their practice in ways which offer every child a more appropriate education.

Supporting musical development in the early years

Linda Pound and Chris Harrison

Open University Press
Buckingham • Philadelphia

Open University Press
Celtic Court
22 Ballmoor
Buckingham
MK18 1XW

email: enquiries@openup.co.uk
world wide web: www.openup.co.uk

and
325 Chestnut Street
Philadelphia, PA 19106, USA

First Published 2003

A catalogue record of this book is available from the British Library

ISBN   0 335 21224 7 (pbk)   0 335 21225 5 (hbk)

Library of Congress Cataloging-in-Publication Data
Pound, Linda.
   Supporting musical development in the early years/Linda Pound and Chris
   Harrison.
      p. cm. – (Supporting early learning)
   Includes bibliographical references and index.
   ISBN 0-335-21225-5 – ISBN 0-335-21224-7 (pbk.)
      1. Music – Instruction and study – Juvenile.   2. Child development.
   3. Education, Elementary.   I. Harrison, Chris.   II. Title.   III. Series.
   MT1.P66   2002
   372.87′049–dc21   2002021400

Typeset by Type Study, Scarborough
Printed in Great Britain by Biddles Ltd, Guildford and King's Lynn

Contents

Series editors' preface

This book is one of a series which will be of interest to all those who are concerned with the care and education of children from birth to 6 years old – childminders, teachers and other professionals in schools; those who work in playgroups, private and community nurseries and similar institutions; governors, providers and managers. We also speak to parents and carers, whose involvement is probably the most influential of all for children's learning and development.

Our focus is on improving the effectiveness of early education. Policy developments come and go, and difficult decisions are often forced on all those with responsibility for young children's well-being. We aim to help with these decisions by showing how developmental approaches to young children's education not only accord with our fundamental educational principles, but provide a positive and sound basis for learning.

Each book recognizes and demonstrates that children from birth to 6 years old have particular developmental learning needs, and that all those providing care and education for them would be wise to approach their work developmentally. This applies just as much to the acquisition of subject knowledge, skills and understanding, as to other educational goals such as social skills, attitudes and dispositions. In this series, there are several volumes with a subject-based focus, and the main aim is to show how that can be introduced to young children within the framework of an integrated and developmentally appropriate curriculum, without losing its integrity as an area of knowledge in its own right. We also stress the importance of providing a learning environment which is carefully planned for children's own active learning. The present volume is, as one might say, in tune with what Confucius maintained as long ago as 500 BC, that 'music produces a pleasure which human nature cannot do without'. The authors also support and promote what Martin Luther, in 1569, said: 'I always loved music; whoso has skill in this art is of a good temperament, fitted for all things. We must teach music in schools: a schoolmaster ought to have skill in music, or I would not regard him.' The inclusion of music, as one of the fundamental arts, has too long been neglected, and this volume gives all adults working with young children a great deal of help in recognizing its importance, and in finding ways of enjoying promoting its development.

Access for all children is fundamental to the provision of educational opportunity. We are concerned to emphasize anti-discriminatory approaches throughout, as well as the importance of recognizing that meeting special educational needs must be an integral purpose of curriculum development and planning. We see the role of play in learning as a central one, and one which also relates to all-round emotional, social and physical development. Play, along with other forms of active learning, is normally a natural point of access to the curriculum for each child at his or her particular stage and level of understanding. It is therefore an essential force in making for equal opportunities in learning, intrinsic as it is to all areas of development. We believe that these two aspects, play and equal opportunities, are so important that we not only highlight them in each volume in this series, but we also include separate volumes on them as well.

Throughout this series, we encourage readers to reflect on the education being offered to young children, by revisiting the developmental principles which most practitioners hold, and using them to analyse their observations of the children. In this way, readers can evaluate ideas about the most effective ways of educating young children, and develop strategies for approaching their practice in ways which exemplify their fundamental educational beliefs, and offer every child a more appropriate education.

The authors of each book in the series subscribe to the following set of principles for a developmental curriculum:

Principles for a developmental curriculum

- Each child is an individual and should be respected and treated as such.
- The early years are a period of development in their own right, and education of young children should be seen as a specialism with its own valid criteria of appropriate practice.

- The role of the educator of young children is to engage actively with what most concerns the child, and to support learning through these preoccupations.
- The educator has a responsibility to foster positive attitudes in children to both self and others, and to counter negative messages which children may have received.
- Each child's cultural and linguistic endowment is seen as the fundamental medium of learning.
- An anti-discriminatory approach is the basis of all respect-worthy education, and is essential as a criterion for a developmentally appropriate curriculum (DAC).
- All children should be offered equal opportunities to progress and develop, and should have equal access to good quality provision. The concepts of multiculturalism and anti-racism are intrinsic to this whole educational approach.
- Partnership with parents should be given priority as the most effective means of ensuring coherence and continuity in children's experiences, and in the curriculum offered to them.
- A democratic perspective permeates education of good quality, and is the basis of transactions between people.

Vicky Hurst and Jenefer Joseph

Acknowledgements

Thanks are due to the staff and children of Robert Owen Early Excellence Centre for their help and support in providing some of the examples described in this book.

Thanks are also due to the archivist at the Froebel Institute for granting permission to use the photograph reproduced in Chapter 3.

Introduction

It is only through music that we have become human.
(Cross 1997, cited in Bannan 2000: 295)

Archaeology from prehistoric sites gives us some indication of the many thousands of years that humans have been engaging in visual representations. We marvel at these but they give little indication of the musical experiences that humans engaged in probably for thousands of years before the onset of visual arts. Current insights from psychology, archaeology and biology are merging to give an insight into the fundamental and primal place of music in human development.

Music has been an important element of the traditions of early childhood education. However, in recent years many practitioners working with young children have been less confident about their own musical abilities and in some cases the role of music in the curriculum has declined. At the same time, young children are constantly surrounded by recorded music in their daily lives – on the radio, on television, in shopping centres, in their toys. This increased access to recorded music has not, however, resulted in a raising of levels of musical achievement and may even have undermined confidence by providing a range of role models to which people think they cannot aspire. Most people now feel themselves to be consumers rather than producers of music and even in the privacy of their own homes, adults may feel inhibited about singing with young children.

In this book, the role of musicality in human development is explored, showing the importance of communication, playfulness and the expression of emotion. The role of music in the early years curriculum is considered and a case is made for ensuring that these three elements are included.

The book is divided into three parts, each of two chapters. In Part 1, we look at the relationship between genetic and environmental factors and their impact on children's musical development. The first chapter considers the evidence for our innate musicality and its functions in human society. It makes the case that all human beings are born with the capacity to make music. In Chapter 2, research studies are summarized to provide an overall picture of children's musical development. The picture is still unclear, and this is an area where further research is needed. Links are made between musical development and other aspects of creative development.

Part 2 focuses on the range of activities and learning experiences that support the development of musical ability. Chapter 3 outlines a music curriculum based on playfulness, communication and the expression of emotion, in which musical improvisation is a central element. Improvisation is often associated with jazz or jamming, but has in fact been an important characteristic of most musical traditions, including the western classical tradition. Chapter 4 describes the ways in which music can be used as a tool for thinking. The relationship between music and other areas of the curriculum is explored. Learning in music both supports and is supported by learning in other areas.

Part 3 considers the role of the adult in supporting music across the curriculum. In Chapter 5 the elements of a music-rich environment, both indoors and out, are described. Chapter 6 emphasizes the role of the adult in planning for and intervening in musical learning.

Part 1

Musical behaviour

Born musical?

If, within western society, it is suggested that everyone is born musical, many people will respond with comments such as, 'well you obviously haven't heard me sing', 'I can't sing a note', 'I'm tone deaf', 'I can't read music', 'I don't play an instrument' or 'I'm just not musically gifted'. And yet, there is good evidence to suggest that music is not, as is widely believed, a gift given only to a few but that we are indeed all born musical. In this chapter, the notion that music is the prerogative of a few musically gifted people will be challenged. Arguments will be put forward to suggest that musicality, far from being a privilege, is something with which we are born and which appears to have a biological purpose in all our lives.

Born gifted?

Music is often thought of as a specialism which is accessible only to a few people who are born with a specific musical talent. Such people are considered to be different from others. The fact that child prodigies exist in music is seen as an argument for seeking out and identifying musical talent at an early age and giving those children specialized training. This reinforces the views of those who are not regarded as gifted that they are completely unmusical and cannot therefore achieve any significant musical success.

Traces of this view can still be seen even in well-respected, recent research. Howard Gardner (1994) developed the idea of multiple intelligences and it is his work that paved the way for Daniel Goleman's (1996) best-selling book *Emotional Intelligence*. Gardner has highlighted a range of intelligences, placing a strong emphasis on symbolic representations. Amongst the seven or eight intelligences which he identifies (Gardner 1999), he lists musical intelligence. Although he recognizes that musical ability develops from a combination of educational, environmental and genetic factors, he does also suggest that 'scholars generally agree that a large portion of musical ability or capacity is inherited' (1994: 187) and that 'there is a sizeable genetic contribution to musical competence' (1994: 188). He further stresses that individual differences in children's musical ability are more marked than in other fields of learning and that training appears to make little difference to the gap between children of various levels of competence. For him, the most compelling argument arises from the musical ability of a small group of autistic children who reflect 'a rhythmic and melodic capacity that is primarily hereditary, and which needs as little external stimulation as does walking or talking in the normal child' (1994: 189).

It is true that a very small group of such children show remarkable abilities, way beyond what even a highly trained professional musician could achieve, but in a very small range of skills. They may, for example, be able to play a full piece of music after just one hearing, from memory and without error. Other *savants* (as they are sometimes termed) show a similar level of competence in drawing or, like the character played by Dustin Hoffman in the film *Rainman*, mathematics.

Born musical?

Many other writers and researchers refute any idea that musical ability is limited to a small number of gifted individuals. There are five main arguments against such a narrow view of musical ability:

- in many cultures, everyone is considered musical;
- musical giftedness does not always run in families;
- exceptional musical ability is not always identified at an early age;
- abilities often identified as demonstrating musical giftedness, such as perfect pitch, are found in many people who consider themselves to be unmusical;
- those who achieve musical success are most often those who have spent more time engaged in musical activity.

Looking at the first of these arguments, ethnomusicology has broadened our understanding of the nature of human musicality. Blacking (1976), for example, shows how, in societies around the world, the expectation is that everyone is musical, that everyone engages in musical activity as part of their day-to-day life. He attacks the way in which, in western societies, music has become an élitist subject, all too often available only to a privileged few:

> If, for example, all members of an African society are able to perform and listen intelligently to their own indigenous music . . . we must ask why apparently general musical abilities should be restricted to a chosen few in societies supposed to be culturally more advanced. Does cultural development represent a real advance in human sensitivity and technical ability, or is it chiefly a diversion for élites and a weapon of class exploitation? Must the majority be made 'unmusical' so that a few may become more 'musical'?
>
> (Blacking 1976: 4)

In an account of the Anang Ibibo of Nigeria, Messenger (1958: 20, cited in Sloboda and Davidson 1996: 176) states:

> We were constantly amazed at the musical abilities displayed by these people, especially by the children who, before the age of 5, can sing hundreds of songs, both individually and in choral groups and, in addition, are able to play several percussion instruments . . . We searched in vain for the 'non-musical' person.

Regarding the second argument, many people point to the existence of musical families as evidence that musical ability is an hereditary trait not possessed by all. The Bach family, who were successful musicians over several generations from the sixteenth to the eighteenth centuries, is a classic example of this phenomenon. We also find generations of folk musicians in the Irish and Scottish traditions. In Mali, musicians have been drawn exclusively from those belonging to *jeli* families (Duran 1999: 541).

However, most renowned composers and performers have not come from families of professional musicians. Haydn was the son of a wheel-wright; Chopin and Schubert were the sons of schoolteachers (Blom 1954). In their study of high-achieving young musicians, Sloboda and Davidson (1996: 180) found that 'the parents of the high achievers were not music performers themselves. Rather, they were, at most, people who enjoyed an amateur interest in music through listening.'

It was not the musical abilities of the parents that made a difference but the high level of support that they gave their children. This interest is reflected in Gardner's (1993a: 113) description of the pianist Artur Rubin-stein's (1887–1982) early introduction to music and the great delight shown by his family (who did not consider themselves to be musical) in his musical abilities:

> As a toddler in Poland, he loved all manner of sounds, including fac-tory sirens, the singing of old Jewish peddlers, and the chants of ice cream sellers. While he refused to speak, he loved to sing and thereby created quite a sensation at home. In fact his abilities soon degener-ated into a sport, where everyone tried to reach him by songs, and he himself came to recognize people by their tunes.

The third argument against the narrow view of musical ability identifies that while some musicians have been child prodigies, most musicians have not shown outstanding early promise. The research of Sloboda and others indicates that very few of the successful musicians in their samples 'displayed any overt signs of musical precocity' (Sloboda and Howe 1991, cited in Sloboda and Davidson 1996: 177). In a few cases, those who have been identified at a young age as having great musical potential are later not seen as having unusual skills. Although Mozart achieved lasting status as a composer, few now have heard of William Crotch (1775–1847), also a child prodigy and once billed as the English Mozart. As his entry in *Grove's Dictionary* states:

> He also proved later on that an abnormally early development of musical genius does not necessarily lead to the highest eminence, at any rate in creative ability.
>
> (Blom 1954: 544)

Perfect pitch, the focus of the fourth argument, is often talked about in hushed tones and widely seen as an indicator of high musical ability.

People are often thought of as possessing some special gift if they can reproduce or identify given notes in the western musical scale. However, current research (Smith 2001) suggests that perfect pitch is something we are all born with, and that it is linked to language learning. In many cases the ability is lost because it is not used in day-to-day life, but in situations where it is of value it is more likely to be retained. Those speaking tonal languages like Vietnamese or Cantonese usually retain the ability, since changing the pitch at which a word is said changes its meaning. Similarly, those who learn an instrument early are more likely to retain the ability and will have been taught to associate pitches with their letter names. Blind people also demonstrate a higher incidence of perfect pitch since they rely on the pitch of a sound to help them to locate its source.

Finally, music research shows that high levels of musical achievement are always preceded by intensive practice. This is consistent with the work of psychologists (such as Sosniak 1985) who suggest that in any area of learning, success is linked to the amount of time spent doing it. If you spend more time reading you will get better at reading; if you spend more time swimming or playing chess you will get better at swimming or playing chess; and if you spend more time making music you will get better at that too. Indeed, Papousek (1994) suggests that as parents sing to their babies, they themselves become better at singing. Researchers (Ericsson *et al.* 1993, cited in Sloboda and Davidson 1996: 183) indicate that professional violinists had accumulated approximately 10,000 hours of practice by the age of 20. Entry to a specialist music school is unlikely to be achieved by anyone having spent less than 5000 hours practising their instrument. This factor more than any other in the musician's background contributed to their success.

None of this rules out the possibility that some children have a greater interest in or aptitude for music than others, but this aptitude will often be the result of greater experience and confidence. It is Sloboda's view that 'differences in accomplishment are mainly due to differences in experience, opportunity and motivation'. As he writes:

> I don't know that all of us could be a Nigel Kennedy, but most of us have much more musical capacity than we believe. Even Mozart had to put in the hours.
>
> (Sloboda, cited in Mihill 1993: 6)

Music: a fundamental human activity

We have seen that, in many cultures around the world, everyone is considered to be musical. We have also seen that musical ability is not limited
to a few people with unusual qualities. It seems, therefore, that the
capacity to make music is something which everyone possesses and can
enjoy. This is underlined by the following facts:

- there is a close relationship between music and the development of the
  brain;
- music serves a number of universal functions in all human cultures;
- music plays a vital role in the care and nurturing of babies.

Music and the brain

New technologies have given researchers new insights into the working
of the brain. For those studying babies and toddlers this is of particular
interest since neuroscience can demonstrate what is happening as early
development occurs. There is enormous interest in the functions of the two
hemispheres of the brain. It is important to remember some facts about
the brain when considering such studies:

- the right hemisphere of the brain is linked to the left side of the body
  and vice versa;
- the left hemisphere is generally associated with speech and with logical
  thought whereas the right hemisphere tends to be linked to a wide
  range of areas including colour, tactile experience and spatial awareness;
- these associations are true for most people; however, in those who are
  left-handed the areas of brain function may be wholly or partly
  reversed.

In relation to music, the left hemisphere is involved in the words of
songs, whereas the right hemisphere is engaged in the tune. Odam (1995:
12) describes the left of the brain as 'the hemisphere that deals with lin-
guistics and logics' and the right as 'that which deals with musical sounds,
intuition and holistic thought'. Thinking and learning are enhanced when
both hemispheres of the brain are stimulated, and music plays a vital role
in this. Odam (1995: 19) draws on a range of research to highlight the role
played by music in the development of the brain: 'Music is a unique
schooling for the brain, involving both right- and left-brain processes
wedded together through fine and disciplined movement.'

The universal functions of music

Language has much in common with music. It is possible that language grew out of music, since as Storr (1992: 12) suggests 'it may even have been the case . . . that human beings danced before they walked'. Vocalization and the use of tools and instruments – or singing and music-making as we might think of it – became possible only once humans could walk. It also seems likely therefore that humans sang long before they talked (Pound 2002, citing Storr 1992 and Blacking 1987).

Music is sometimes described as a universal language. This claim is probably exaggerated since the conventions of music vary from culture to culture in much the same way as spoken languages do. This has long been clear to ethnomusicologists looking at different cultural traditions. Seeger, for example, wrote in 1941 (cited in Merriam 1964: 10):

> We must, of course, be careful to avoid the fallacy that music is a 'universal language'. There are many music communities in the world, though not, probably, as many as there are speech communities. Many of them are mutually unintelligible.

However, there are some similarities and it is certainly true that music (like language) serves a number of common functions in all cultures. Gregory (1997) identifies a wide range of traditional roles of music, including lullabies, games, work music, healing, dancing and storytelling. For the purposes of this book, the functions of music have been summarized as follows:

- to create atmosphere or mood;
- to support group identity;
- to support memory;
- to communicate in situations where it may otherwise be difficult.

Looking at the first of these functions, music is widely used to evoke particular moods or atmospheres. As part of religious ceremonies and acts of worship or celebration, music is used to reflect or create the desired mood. Lullabies are used in all cultures to create a calm, soothing, sleep-inducing atmosphere. Even in supermarkets, managers are aware of this and play music to encourage shoppers to linger and spend more money.

Recent theories (Devereux 2001) suggest that even in prehistoric times, priests or ceremonial leaders were aware of the power of music to create a mystical atmosphere. Stone structures like Maes Howe in Orkney and Newgrange in Ireland were, he suggests, built 5000 years ago to shape the sounds produced by instrument or voice in a manner that produced a great sense of awe in the listener.

Second, music has traditionally played a strong role in supporting group cohesion. Football teams have songs and chants which draw their supporters together in a sense of group identity. School songs, national anthems and regimental marches are designed to have much the same effect – creating, it is hoped, a sense of togetherness. Groups of workers developed work-songs over the centuries to enable them to work more rhythmically and efficiently and to ease the burden of toil. Groups of young people closely identify with particular styles of pop music as part of their social identity.

Third, songs and music make it easier for us to remember things. Advertisers are only too well aware of this – their advertising jingles becoming slogans for children to chant over and over again. Children recite the alphabet, for example, more readily when it is set to music. Counting songs help children to remember the order in which numbers must be used if counting is to be accurate and it is, of course, possible to buy audio tapes in which the times tables are set to music in order to help children memorize them.

At a more fundamental level, songs and rhythmic poetry have been used through the ages to convey information from one generation to another. In his fascinating description of Australian aboriginal life entitled *Songlines*, Bruce Chatwin (1987: 120) writes about the way in which traditional songs describe the surrounding landscape. He records the words of Arkady, a researcher into aboriginal culture, who remarks that 'music . . . is a memory bank for finding one's way about the world'. All over the world, legends, which contain the history of a nation or cultural group, are set to music in the form of ballads, making the information more memorable. The epic song *Sunjata* which tells the story of the thirteenth-century ruler of Mali 'is still today the most important in every traditional musician's repertoire' (Duran 1999: 540).

Egan (1991) reinforces this view by putting forward a theory that, since music is used in this way by cultures which do not use written forms, it is of particular value for young children who are, by their nature, not yet literate. This is not to trivialize music but to recognize that it has been used by humans for countless ages as an important tool for thinking.

Finally, Papousek (1994) asserts that one of the important biological functions of music is to communicate ideas which might be difficult to express in any other way. This might refer to difficulties of distance. Yodelling, for example, has developed to allow communication over difficult mountainous terrain. On a more mundane level, adults often use a sing-song voice when calling their children from a distance. For example, we might sing out a two-note chant such as *Mary-Lou, where are you? Mary-Lou, where are you?* or *It's dinner time, dinner time, dinner time!* when children are at some distance from us.

More commonly our use of music reflects difficulty in expressing emotions. The musical repertoires of most, if not all, cultures abound with love songs, for example. We can sing about love in a way which we might find more difficult to express in conversation. Victor Hugo, the nineteenth-century French poet, expressed this view in the words 'music expresses that which cannot be said and on which it is impossible to be silent' (cited in Exley 1991). Tolstoy called music 'the shorthand of emotion' (cited in Exley 1991) and Chatwin (1987) underlines the way in which extremes of emotion such as anger and joy are vented through music.

The role of music in the care and nurturing of babies

It is these difficulties of emotion and, perhaps metaphorically at least, distance which music helps us to address when we are dealing with very young babies and children. Small babies are distanced from us in the sense that they have not yet been drawn into our culture and are unaware of emotions as identifiable states. Therefore communication is difficult and music supports adults in reducing the distance and highlighting emotions. Music and musical elements are, therefore, vital to the early social development of babies. Since musical elements can be traced through different species, it is suggested that music must have a biological function, integral to human development. Papousek and Papousek (1994: 45) write:

> Musical engagement has mostly been considered as a cultural contribution to child-rearing. However, the present evidence on involvement of musical interchanges in parent–infant interactions during the pre-verbal age sharpens our attention to potential biological origins of musicality.

Babies are born with social and communicative competence which is developed by adults through the use of music. The structure of songs and style of language used by carers (or *motherese* as it is often termed) have, as we will see in this chapter, many universal characteristics and draw on the innate musicality of both adults and children. Adults work to bring the baby into their culture, using music to:

- capture the baby's attention, gradually shifting perception from a sensory to a cognitive process for learning and developing;
- develop shared meaning through non-verbal communication and, as it develops, spoken language;
- express and communicate feelings and emotions.

Capturing the baby's attention

In their earliest interactions with babies, parents and other members of the baby's immediate circle, both young and old, make use of musical elements in order to capture the baby's attention. Even very young children, barely past babyhood themselves, do this (Dunn 1988). We imitate the sounds made by babies and repeat them, sometimes raising the pitch, sometimes lowering it, sometimes speaking very slowly, sometimes making short rapid sounds. In playing in this way, the sounds the baby produces – often by chance – are made more obvious or noticeable and in turn the baby repeats something of what he or she hears. The adult again picks up the sound and plays with it. Just watch as people meet a new baby for the first time to see this pattern in action. We respond to the baby's voice so rapidly that it can only be an unconscious process, something we are hard-wired to do (Papousek and Papousek 1994). Karmiloff-Smith (1994: 40) quotes a mother who is commenting on this type of interaction:

> I keep trying to speak to her normally – but it's odd, I find myself quite naturally speaking in a sing-song voice whenever I'm with her. When one of my friends is here, I try to talk normally. You feel such an idiot. Somehow it just comes out, like there was a special language for babies that we never have to learn. I've noticed people in the street do it too. The newsagent does it the most – a real piece of opera whenever he sees Evelyn.

What is of particular interest in this mother's words is her recognition of the language that we use with babies as being one which 'we never have to learn'.

Babies have learnt something about sound before birth. They have probably not heard precisely what we hear but will have been surrounded by sounds – muffled by their protective uterine wall and dominated by the beat of the mother's heart. The timbre of the mother's voice, the intonation of her preferred language and the changing rhythms of her body as she rests and moves will have been perceived by the unborn infant. At birth they have a preference for the sound of their mother's voice, or failing that, the voice of someone speaking their mother's first language. They will respond to tunes made familiar through the pregnancy, listened to frequently by their mother (Eliot 1999). They also have an ability which will slowly be lost: an ability to distinguish all the sounds in all the languages that exist (Smith and Cowie 1988). Frequent exposure to just one or two languages gradually reduces their ability to the point where they can distinguish only between the range of sounds used in the language or languages of the home.

Contrary to general belief, newborn babies seem to enjoy complex sounds. Eliot (1999: 228) writes:

In contrast to vision, where newborns show a distinct preference for simpler stimuli, their hearing preferences tilt towards the more complex, and music or highly intonated speech fills the bill better than pure tones or other simple sounds.

Developing shared meaning

Another important factor in this kind of play is the fact that adults respond to the baby's vocalizations as though the baby intends to communicate something (Wells and Nicholls 1985). We interpret their exploratory or musical sounds as attempts at communication. Hearing these early utterances, we respond as though the baby had said that they are hungry or thirsty or need changing and then proceed to soothe these perceived worries. What babies learn from this is the two-way process of communication (although initially adults temporarily take both parts) and the tune or intonation of the language. We ask the question which expresses what we think the child might be trying to communicate and then answer the question – carrying both sides of the conversation. These interactions are sometimes called protoconversations (Trevarthen and Marwick 1986).

Fernald (1992) has demonstrated the way in which particular tunes or intonations are used by parents or carers to represent different emotions. As Figure 1.1 shows, very similar sound patterns or intonations are used in different languages to express soothing sentiments, approval or denial. Although most of these studies have focused on European languages and American use of English, there is some evidence that these apparently universal representations are used in other languages. Indeed, there is an indication that it holds true in Mandarin, a tonal language which relies for meaning not simply on syllables but on the pitch at which those syllables are produced. Chinese caregivers uttering the baby word for mother will choose a tone which completely changes the meaning of the word in order to maintain the universal tune.

The universal nature of some musical phrases can extend well into childhood. Bernstein (cited in Storr 1992: 59) suggests that children all around the world use the teasing taunt *nah-nah-ni-nah-nah* (sung to the equivalent notes G, E, A, G, E).

Communicating feelings: baby songs and dances

From around 3 or 4 months of age, parents play games with babies that have an important role in their developing communication with others. Moreover these games draw the infant into the culture of the family or

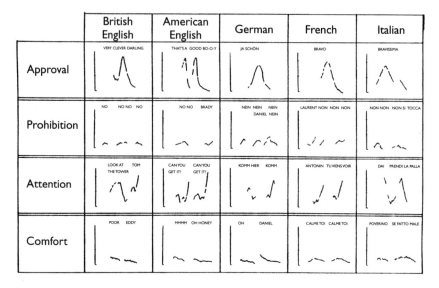

Figure 1.1 Shapes of pitch contours from mothers' speech to 12-month-old infants.
Source: Fernald 1992: 401.

community. Trevarthen (1998) describes the shift from protoconversations to games involving traditional rhymes, songs and chants. He writes of the lively character, suspense and changes in tempo which characterize these nursery songs or chants. In his earlier writing, Trevarthen (1989) suggested that tradition supplies the mother with rhymes, songs and nursery chants that have a clear vocal line accompanied by actions. More recently he states that:

> we have found that mothers do not restrict their entertainments to traditional ditties. Many perform dance and song for their babies using their own favourite rock or folk music, in forms that exhibit the same universal features as those made for babies, especially in the ways in which they are made by a happy mother. Babies are introduced very early to the popular music of the day.
>
> (Trevarthen 1998: 92)

What characterizes these songs is that:

- 'the temporal or musical form of these "baby songs" and "baby dances" appears to be essentially the same in very different cultures, regardless of their different languages' (Trevarthen 1987: 189);

- they stimulate interest, through repeated movement, changes in tempo and pitch. A traditional example might be *This is the way the ladies ride* . . . with its varied tempo depicting different riders;
- they invite an emotional response, such as dread or laughter. The anticipation of such emotions in the song means that the baby is paying attention to rhythm and melody;
- they share a story-like structure involving an introduction, development or build-up and climax or resolution (Trevarthen 1998). *Walking round the garden like a teddy bear* offers an example of the structure.

The importance of emotions

The importance of emotional development has been increasingly recognized, not just as part of personal development, important as this is, but also as a crucial part of cognitive development (Goleman 1996; LeDoux 1999). The role of emotions includes a contribution to the following aspects of learning and development (based on Pound 2001: 126):

- making babies aware of the world around them (Trevarthen 1979);
- making things memorable – thus reinforcing learning not just in infancy but also throughout life (Siegel 1999: 51);
- coordinating activities (Siegel 1999: 210) by stimulating both sides of the brain and preparing the brain and the rest of the body for action (Siegel 1999: 124);
- helping us to 'appreciate art, make lasting friendships or even . . . to choose which box of cereals to buy' (Eliot 1999: 294);
- establishing the critical foundation on which every other mental skill can flourish (Eliot 1999: 290);
- 'allowing one person to have a sense of the mental state of another' (Siegel 1999: 148).

Musical elements have an important part to play in the development and communication of emotional responses, as in other situations where communication is difficult and words alone are not sufficient to convey what is meant. As Siegel (1999: 152) reminds us: 'music has been described as one of the purest expressions of emotions that exists.' Adult memories of their musical experiences in early childhood are described by Lundin and Sandberg (2001: 247) and they emphasize the role of music in 'creating warmth, partnership, community, attention and atmosphere'.

Emotion is expressed as part of mothers' interactions with their babies described above, in their protoconversations. It is also achieved by the use of song to create atmosphere. Lullabies are the most obvious example of this – their lilting style lulling the baby to sleep. But emotion is also reflected for young children through a wide range of songs and rhymes. The excitement that is engendered as the speed of the song is accelerated or the fear as the pace is slowed down to the point where everything stops . . . but the listener knows that the structure is incomplete and waits expectantly for the closing line. Adding actions to these musical interactions promotes the engagement of the brain – the ensuing *mass action* (Carter 1998: 11) making learning more likely to occur. Eliot (1999: 156) similarly suggests that vestibular stimulation – rocking, swaying, swinging, jiggling and bouncing – 'is not only soothing . . . it is actually quite good for [the] emerging mind!'

Music and playfulness

Playful exchanges such as those engaged in by parents and infants are clearly teaching the infant about communication, social and linguistic interaction. Their importance is, however, equally great in encouraging the baby to develop the creativity which humans need in order to adapt and change in line with the constantly evolving environment which we have created for ourselves (Pound 2002). Whereas other animals can often rely on reflex action, humans need to think (sometimes on their feet) and problem-solve in ever-changing contexts. Such resourcefulness is dependent on 'a long and playful childhood' (Pound 2002: 23). The babbling which babies engage in from their earliest months is a form of play which Papousek (1994) underlines in referring to the baby's voice as the first toy. In his view, playfulness, creativity and musicality go hand in hand and have a direct evolutionary, biological purpose.

Song-like and dance-like performances frequently accompany children's playful activity in the first year of life. Trevarthen (1998) suggests that the infant, from as early as 6 months old, may be working to create a playful learning environment with those with whom he or she interacts. The positive emotional climate developed in this way has the added bonus of producing in the brain the optimum chemical environment for learning to take place.

The repertoire of songs developed between child and caregiver allows the child to play at experiencing different emotions, almost at will. The young child's demands for repeat performances of favourite songs indicate the way in which they enjoy feeling over and over again the fear, happiness or anticipation that songs can engender.

Conclusion

There is good evidence to support the view that we are born musical. Even before we are born, music has an impact on our lives and stimulates our development. From birth, we develop our musical awareness through communication, the expression of emotion and playfulness. In turn, musical activity helps us to develop our capacity to communicate with others, to express our feelings and to play. It is no accident that we use the term 'play' as the main way of referring to someone's engagement in musical activity.

Musical development

In the previous chapter, we looked at innate musical understandings. In this chapter the development of musical competence is explored. Views of how musical competence develop vary widely because:

- different researchers and theorists hold different views of what counts as music;
- musical development depends on a wide range of factors;
- views of children as learners have changed.

What counts as music?

In this book we are using Blacking's (1976) definition of music as 'humanly organised sound'. This wide definition is helpful because we are looking at the development of musical competence in all human beings, and we wish to encompass all kinds of music-making. Music education has often focused on developing the skills needed to perform in the western classical tradition, but music is, in reality, much more than that. Music plays an important part in all our adult lives and we need to prepare children to take part in a whole range of musical activities. As Christopher Small (1998) reminds us, music, or 'musicking', includes the symphony orchestra, supermarket music, rock groups, jazz musicians, church organists, and people singing at public events or even to themselves while doing routine tasks.

Factors influencing development

Children's development depends on a wide range of factors, which are defined by different writers in different ways. Welch (1998: 28) lists the factors involved as 'basic biological potential, maturation, experience, opportunity, interest, education, family, peers, and socio-cultural context'. As indicated in Chapter 1, Sloboda (Mihill 1993) defines the influencing factors as experience, opportunity and motivation. Other researchers (Blacking 1995; Trevarthen 1998) stress the role of enculturation, or the influence of the child's cultural experience on their musical development. Just as language develops in response to the dominant language of the home and the wider community, so musical development reflects the music that is heard in the home environment or culture. Dyson (2001: 30) describes an interaction between two 6-year-old girls which shows how there can be a gap between school and home cultures:

> One day Denise and Vanessa collaboratively wrote a short R&B song by re-voicing popular lyrics. The resulting product, however, never saw the official stage, in part because, as Denise said, Rita (the teacher) probably wasn't 'used' to this style of song. 'Teen-age-er' songs were part of the children's unofficial play, glamorized futures – and adults (including their parents) voiced concerns.

Learning and development are affected by the nature of teaching and adult intervention. Some of the apparent discrepancies between accounts of children's musical development may reflect differences in the educational environment. Understandings of literacy were radically changed by studies of children who appeared to learn unaided (Clark 1976). Few such studies exist in relation to music and we are only just beginning to learn about possible levels of competence and how they are achieved.

Views of children as learners

There have been enormous developments in research techniques enabling researchers to gain better insight into the workings of children's minds and their intentions. At the same time there has been a shift in developmental psychology which has led to an emphasis on what children actually can do and their competence as learners, replacing an earlier emphasis on their limited achievements against an absolute model. The fact that a child cannot, for example, repeat a whole song does not mean that they have not heard parts of the melody or understood its structure.

We also need to take account of the fact that patterns of development vary widely from child to child, adult to adult.

What do we know about children's musical development?

Many researchers have produced findings which have been related to specific age groups. We summarize these below, but it should be emphasized that they are general stages in development, rather than age-specific behaviours. Furthermore, most of this research has been conducted in Europe and North America and does not reflect the wide cultural variation that exists around the world. It may underestimate young children's potential to an even greater extent, as examples from some cultures show that where there is a focus on music in early childhood, children achieve extensive levels of competence at an early age. The following summary by Gardner (1993a: 109, citing Messenger 1958) describing the Anang of Nigeria illustrates this:

> Infants scarcely a week old are introduced to music and dancing by their mothers. Fathers fashion small drums for their children. When they reach the age of two, children join groups where they learn many basic cultural skills, including singing, dancing, and playing of instruments. By the age of five, the young Anang can sing hundreds of songs, play several percussion instruments, and perform dozens of intricate dance movements.

As you read the sections that follow, you should remain aware that what is described is a general direction of development, rather than a precise chronological mapping. Young learners find their own routes and this may result in a pattern of development that looks quite different from what is described below. Some children with disabilities or special educational needs may take longer to go through some of these phases of development. Others may move rapidly through some early phases or develop slowly at first but progress faster later.

The first year of life

Babies babble and enjoy engaging in vocal play (Hargreaves and Galton 1992; Papousek 1994; Duffy 1998). As indicated in Chapter 1, parents and other caregivers weave an interactive song and dance with babies – as they imitate the sounds that the baby makes and are in turn imitated by the infant. The imitation of movements may be less apparent but is clearly evident in videotapes, where synchronous movement between babies and caregivers is a feature of the dance-like interactions between adult and infant from the baby's earliest days. This behaviour marks the beginning of the complicated balance between the child's innate behaviour and the impact of the environment as their first sounds are encouraged or ignored by those around them. The level and style of interaction is shaped as much by the baby's response as by the adults' level of engagement (Trevarthen 1998).

Babies of this age demonstrate a number of other competences (Trehub *et al.* 1997). Infants enjoy listening to music, are sensitive to melodic contour and musical intervals, alert to some properties of harmony, and demonstrate some musical preferences. They show preferences for music listened to by their mothers during the later stages of pregnancy, and perhaps, even more surprisingly, prefer the sound of stories read by their mothers at that time to other similar stories. Eliot (1999) describes an experiment in which expectant mothers were asked to read aloud *The Cat in the Hat* by Dr Seuss for a total of five hours during the last six weeks of their pregnancy. Very soon after birth, the newborn babies preferred to hear their mothers read the same story, distinguishing it from other stories, even being able to differentiate it from other stories by the same author.

A number of writers and researchers (Shuter-Dyson and Gabriel 1981; Gardner 1994; Duffy 1998) agree that, even at this young age, babies are alert to musical stimuli, such as changes in the speed or other qualities of the sounds they hear. They respond especially well to songs with simple musical themes and a strong regular pulse (Gardner 1994). They associate sounds with the objects that make them, such as the sound of a spoon on a cup or a dish (Duffy 1998). These responses to the sounds around them are often demonstrated through their movements, dances and gestures.

Gardner (1993a: 108) proposes a 'rough-and-ready portrait of early musical competence':

> During infancy normal (sic) children sing as well as babble: they can emit individual sounds, produce undulating patterns, and even imitate prosodic patterns and tones sung by others with better than random accuracy . . . Infants as young as two months old are able to match the pitch, loudness, and melodic contour of their mother's songs, and . . . infants at four months can match rhythmic structure as well . . . They can also engage in sound play that clearly exhibits creative, or generative, properties.

From 1 to 2 years of age

The second year of life is characterized by the demonstration of an increasingly wide range of spontaneous music-making. Gardner (1993a: 109) reminds us that:

> For the first time, they begin on their own to emit series of punctate tones that explore various small intervals; seconds, minor thirds, major thirds, and fourths. They invent spontaneous songs that prove difficult to notate; and, before long, they begin to produce small sections ('characteristic bits') of familiar songs heard around them – such as the 'EI-EI-O' from 'Old Macdonald' or 'All fall down' from 'Ring around the Rosie'.

In other words, while continuing to make gliding vocal sounds, toddlers also begin to introduce more distinct pitches, and to take small steps from note to note. The 'characteristic bits' are sometimes used to label or identify a song. Lukas, for example, wanted his key worker to sing *Miss Polly had a Dolly*. He asked for 'sick, sick', which the practitioner was able to identify and she began to sing the song for him. He joined in with some of the actions by rocking his arms, and with some of the words, particularly 'sick, sick, sick'.

At this age, children begin to be able to take a song or another musical pattern and play with it (Gardner 1994), in much the same way as they play with words (Weir 1962). They enjoy emphasizing the rhythm, playing with particular combinations of notes and repeating particular syllables. Interestingly, such observations show that children are often able to use words in songs that they are unable to use in conversation.

Most children of this age are able to walk and run, and their response to music may be characterized by jumping or bouncing. In addition, they like joining in with adults or peers making music. Their interest is often demonstrated through dancing, clapping, swaying and swinging their arms or bobbing up and down in time to the music. Shauna swayed gently as another child explored the musical instruments in another part of the room. Children of this age also show increasing interest in making sounds with everyday objects and materials, including musical instruments. Marlon, like so many other children of this age, enjoys banging saucepans and lids, and smiles broadly with satisfaction at the sounds he creates.

John displays many of the characteristics of children at this early stage of increasingly deliberate and conscious music-making. On his first day back at nursery after two weeks away, he heard music playing in another room and immediately went to find the source of the music. He joined in the dancing enthusiastically, showing his keen interest in music and dancing by leaving his base room. He moved rhythmically to the music, watching the adults dancing and starting to clap when they clapped in time to the music. On another occasion he was playing with a small keyboard. When he pressed the keys it automatically played *Twinkle, Twinkle Little Star*. Staff began singing the words and John continued to press the keys.

In this way he was able to enjoy the sense of involvement in accompanying the singing and to encourage the adults to carry on singing. *Twinkle, Twinkle Little Star* became a firm favourite for John over several days and although his day-to-day speech was sometimes difficult to interpret, he was able to sing many of the words to the song clearly and confidently.

From 2 to 3 years of age

As their physical coordination develops, children of this age are able to explore the sound potential of toys and other household objects in a more sustained and deliberate fashion (Duffy 1998). Gabriella and Max were playing at the water tray and giggled conspiratorially as they managed to make a series of funny sounds with pieces of tubing and funnels. Max moved on later the same day to experiment in a similar way with instruments. He was exploring what could be done with a small keyboard. He used his fingers separately to press down individual keys. Then he used the palm of his hand to press down several keys at once. He then took a toy fish which happened to be beside the keyboard and pressed that on the keys. He used the tail of the fish to play individual keys and placed the fish flat on the keys in order to play several notes at the same time. After several minutes, he returned to using his fingers to press individual keys, moving systematically along the keyboard from the lowest to the highest notes. He then made several bangs on the keyboard with his whole hand. He carried the keyboard over to the piano, briefly repeated some of the same actions on the piano and then moved off to play with cars.

Children of this age enjoy clapping as an expression of rhythm. Their clapping is not always accurate, but inaccuracies are usually due to the limitations of their motor control rather than lack of understanding. Trevarthen (1989) emphasizes the inherent sense of rhythm demonstrated even in the first year of life. As coordination increases, children are able to join in with action rhymes and respond through movement to different tempos in music. They can match movements to music for short periods of time and can imitate short parts of tunes accurately (Moog 1976).

At this age, young children build on their growing ability to take 'characteristic bits' of familiar songs, using longer phrases. These are often used to support something else they are engaged in. Oliver, playing with a small construction set which included some bricks and ladders began quietly to sing *Bob the Builder* to himself. This play lasted for several minutes, and during that time he sang the whole song. The contrast seen in younger children between the language used in speech and that which they are able to reproduce in singing continues to be apparent at this stage. Rachael blew out the candles on her pretend cake in the home corner and sang the words to *Happy Birthday to You*. However, when a member of staff approached, she said, 'make cake for party'.

Their interest in playing with known songs and rhythms continues, and invented songs emerge. Harry was playing with plastic dinosaurs. As he walked them over plastic grass and between cardboard trees he started to sing one of his favourite songs, *Walking through the Jungle*. He added a verse of his own invention: 'I thought I saw a dinosaur . . .'.

Gardner (1994) cites the work of Heinz Werner in 1917 who studied young children's spontaneous melodies. He suggests that between the ages of 2 and 3 years, children's spontaneous vocalizations usually include descending melodies ending on the lowest note.

An interesting parallel with the development of drawing is seen in children's early attempts at singing songs. In the same way as heads and feet appear in children's drawings before the middle of the body is represented (Wales 1990), so the beginnings and ends of tunes are often reproduced before the middle of the song can be reliably recalled. Sundin (1997: 55) also links children's graphic and musical inventions, offering a delightful summary of young children's spontaneous songs:

> The first singing forms are vague, 'floating' and can be compared to scribbles. Songs from the adult world come in early but are usually 'reproduced' in a compressed or in other ways changed form. From the age of two to three years onward the formula-song (chant) is the dominant type in children's groups, so dominant that . . . it (has been called) *the musical mother tongue* . . . Through these songs the child can communicate and feel solidarity and belongingness with other children. They are the expressions of a linguistic code peculiar to the children's own culture and give rhythm and form to their play.
>
> These songs are usually short, but can change into long, teasing sessions. They can accompany different activities or be a part of them. They may be monotonous to adult ears, repeating a few formulas over and over again, but on closer listening they show considerable variation.

From 3 to 4 years of age

At this age, exploration and experimentation with voice, instruments and other sound-makers continue. Tyler, for example, was interested in the patterns he was able to create with bells. In the home corner, Bryan and Ben used wooden spoons and other utensils to set up a variety of rhythms. Ben used a rolling pin as a microphone and accompanied the spontaneous music-making with rap-like words. Specialist electronic equipment like soundbeam enables children to explore in specific ways, and to develop a sense of control as they discover ways in which they can change the sounds they hear through the movements they make.

There is an increased interest in songs drawn from the home culture. Children enjoy repeating familiar songs, and their increasing vocal stamina and control enable them to reproduce whole songs – although, as we have seen, this may also happen at an earlier stage. Initially, children's singing may be accurate in relation to rhythm and the contours of the tune, and may demonstrate a growing understanding of the overall plan of the melody (Shuter-Dyson and Gabriel 1981). Studies have shown that almost half of children of this age can recognize familiar songs when played without words (Moog 1976; Sloboda 1985).

Children's spontaneous songs get longer, with more use of ascending as well as descending melody lines (Werner, cited in Gardner 1994). Three-year-olds may produce songs lasting up to several minutes. These may be collages of material from existing songs and generally have a free structure with little obvious sense of overall organization (Moog 1976). Sloboda (1985: 205, citing Moog 1976) describes these songs as 'pot-pourri' and says: 'words, melodic lines, and rhythms are mixed up, altered, taken apart and put together again in a different way and then fitted in between stretches of "original ideas".'

As Chloe played by herself she heard an adult in another room leading the singing of *How Do You Do?* She responded by singing to the same tune, while continuing to play the imaginative game in which she was engaged:

Yes she's happy, happy
Happy, happy, happy
HAPPY, very, very happy.

At the same time, increasing physical coordination enables children to demonstrate awareness of beat and tempo through activities such as marching in time to music. Shey, aged 4, enjoys dancing. His rhythmic upper body movements, as he danced to Roxy Music using upper torso, hands and arms, were much admired by other children who pulled up chairs to watch him. However, when a small group of girls who go to ballet classes requested *Swan Lake*, he happily joined in with that too. The group swayed gently and two boys joined them, not in dancing, but in using quiet instruments to accompany the dance. At this age, as many children enter institutional settings for the first time, it is likely that boys and girls will often stereotype their own actions. They are only just beginning to work out what it means to be a boy or a girl. While adults must understand this tendency it is also important that children do not become locked into specific roles but, like Shey, feel able to follow their own interests and to learn from others through working and playing together. (This topic is developed further in Chapter 6.)

Much of what children are able to demonstrate during their first four years of life is dependent on their level of physical or vocal coordination. Swanwick and Tillman (1986), whose work has been influential in providing a framework for the understanding of musical development, describe this stage of development (roughly from birth to 4 years of age) as *mastery*. This implies that the technical preoccupations are more important for children than expressive, communicative or exploratory activity, whereas, as we have seen in the previous chapter, what motivates young children is the drive to express emotions and feelings, to communicate with others and to play both with sounds and with ideas.

The emphasis in Swanwick and Tillman's research was on children's instrumental compositions and it included relatively few vocal examples. There are two considerations we should bear in mind when considering this research. As in most areas of research with young children, structured situations do not always reflect the competence that children are able to demonstrate in playful or meaningful situations. Although they may be grappling with the physical problems of managing instruments or controlling their voices, this does not mean that their actions are not expressive in intention. Children's music-making is limited by their level of motor control: their level of understanding often far exceeds that which they are able to demonstrate. When freed from the need to control instruments, children may demonstrate a higher level of understanding as Glover (1993, cited in Young and Glover 1998: 118–19) describes:

> Composing with the voice has the substantial advantage that children can tap directly into their musical sense, without the difficulty of managing to control sound produced externally on an instrument . . . As a result . . . children's early song compositions are usually much more advanced musically than their instrumental pieces.

From 4 to 5 years of age

Children's technical competence continues to develop. Children of this age can often clap in time to a song (Sloboda 1985) or clap back simple rhythms (Shuter-Dyson and Gabriel 1981). Their dance increasingly demonstrates a growing awareness of rhythm through a growing range of interpretative movements. Children sing with greater accuracy of pitch and are more able to sustain a song in a single key (Sloboda 1985). A majority of children now recognize familiar tunes without their words (Sloboda 1985). At this age, children can enjoy listening to recorded music, and are increasing their knowledge about music, such as the names of some instruments (Duffy 1998). They are also developing a musical vocabulary and are able to use words such as high, low, long, short, fast, slow to describe music (Duffy 1998). Children's progress in these areas of knowledge will vary considerably as it relies heavily on their experience of live music and opportunities for discussion with adults and peers. Whereas some children may comment that a piece of electronic music 'sounds like pianos and violins playing', other children may draw less on technical vocabulary but emphasize imagery. Shey likened the ending of Ravel's *Bolero* to 'the sad bit where she ate the apple and died'.

The research findings outlined above are reflected in the expectations of the *Curriculum Guidance for the Foundation Stage* (QCA 2000: 122), which indicates that, by the age of 5, most children will be able to 'recognise and explore how sounds can be changed, sing simple songs from memory, recognise repeated sounds and sound patterns and match movements to music'.

At this age, children enjoy singing in groups or alone and are developing a large repertoire of familiar songs (Gardner 1994). As their experience of these songs increases, their willingness to create their own spontaneous songs has been observed to decline (Sloboda 1985). There are a number of possible reasons for this:

- Children may wish to avoid error. Similar avoidance is seen in some children's early attempts at writing. Although some are happy to have a go at writing, coming up with highly communicative writing based on their own invented spellings, other children find it very difficult to produce writing which does not match standard forms.
- Gardner (1993b) suggests that children may become obsessed with fine detail and are less concerned with freely exploring the 'big picture'. They are, he argues, less interested in their songs than in reproducing known words and tunes.
- Children enjoy frequent repetition of the same song. This is familiar in children's enjoyment of repeated readings of the same story. They also like to rehearse familiar songs with prescribed movements. Spontaneous or improvised songs are, by definition, harder to repeat in the same way, over and over again.

When Matthew requested Bob the Builder's *Mambo No. 5*, a group of children gathered and attempted to follow the dance steps set out in the song. Their emphasis on getting it right, their interest in small details and their desire to repeat the same sequence in the same way, illustrates all the above characteristics.

While adults can recognize and support children in these endeavours, it is important that children are also given encouragement to work in more creatively demanding ways. Sundin (1997: 48) comments on this aspect of music:

> What . . . struck me was the opposite meaning of two related concepts: children's songs (songs made by adults for children) and children's drawings (drawings made by children). Why was singing considered a reproducing activity and scribbling and drawing a creative one? What did this difference say about our concept of music?

This view is echoed in a story related by Hildebrandt (1998: 68) who asks practitioners a similar question:

> The other day I heard a wonderful song by a four-year-old boy who was getting his hair cut at the mall. When his haircut was over, he burst into a spirited improvisation: 'Ya, ya, ya, ya . . .'
> The hairstylist said, 'Can you sing me a song? What's that song you're singing? Is it Humpty Dumpty?' (It didn't sound remotely like Humpty Dumpty.) 'What songs do you know? Can you sing me a song that you know?'
> The little boy kept on singing and the hairstylist kept asking him for a song.
> Finally I said, 'Maybe he's singing his own song. Sometimes kids make up their own songs.'
> Like the hairstylist, we don't always appreciate children's invented songs as music. Although we strive to honor and encourage children's creativity in all areas of development, sometimes music gets lost in the process. What are we, as early childhood educators, doing to encourage children's creativity in music?

As the work of Coral Davies (1992, 1994, 1997) shows, when children receive encouragement and support, they do continue to produce their own songs. She suggests that 'this improvised song-making seems to die out as children enter school. But perhaps this is only because we do not expect it to continue' (Davies 1997: 15). Other writers share this view. As long ago as 1917, Werner (cited in Gardner 1994) found that the songs of children of this age showed an increased sense of structure, for instance in the use of repeated sections. The work of Davies (1992) and Barrett (1996, cited by Sundin 1997) shows that 5-year-olds can and do invent organized songs. Sundin (1997) goes even further. He refutes the idea (put forward by Kratus (1994)) that children may not be able to compose until about 9 years of age and underlines the way in which children create their own songs long before the age of 5.

From 5 to 7 years of age

Gardner (1994: 196) suggests that there is an 'important convergence among researchers on the importance of the ages 6 to 7 in musical development'. He cites Revesz (1954: 175) in describing 'a gradual transition from playful music-making to a conscious assimilation and correct reproduction' of music, such as trying to play familiar tunes. Welch (1998) describes a study of children's singing competence at 5, 6 and 7 years of age. He suggests that, over the period involved, children's ability to reproduce the words of songs increased significantly year on year. Their ability to pitch the tunes of the songs accurately lagged significantly behind word accuracy. Indeed, significant improvements in accurate pitch were not generally seen until the final year of the study. These findings are interesting when compared with studies of adults, who in general find it easier to remember the tunes rather than the words of songs.

Hargreaves and Galton (1992) refer to the *schematic* stage (which they suggest lasts from 5 to 8 years of age) in which there is an emphasis in their invented work on reproducing the conventions of familiar music. Swanwick and Tillman (1986) similarly describe the stage from 4 to 9 years of age as *imitation*, in which there is a move 'towards socially shared vernacular conventions' (Swanwick 1988: 66). This may be the result of changes in children's lives, such as the introduction of compulsory schooling, rather than a 'natural' development. Children do become more aware of the cultural conventions of the music they hear, and develop an increased ability to recognize changes in tonal melodies (Zenatti 1969, cited in Sloboda 1985: 210; Shuter-Dyson and Gabriel 1981). They are also able to identify the same tune played at different speeds (Sloboda 1985). Their growing musical competence is shown in an increased ability to sing in tune, to control dynamics, and to perform and respond rhythmically and in time.

However, children's creativity and originality can still be fostered and developed. A valuable insight into children's musical understanding and creativity at this age is provided by the research of Coral Davies (1992, 1994, 1997) into children's composed and improvised songs. Her research focuses on children at Key Stage 1 and she identifies three types of song and their characteristics:

- Story songs, where the emphasis is on the narrative and the melodies follow the pattern of the words and may have a loose musical structure.
- Frame songs in which there is a recognizable musical structure often

derived from familiar songs, such as *The Wheels on the Bus.* Although Oscar is only 4, his song shows a grasp of structural features reminiscent of nursery songs, with a linear structure, repetition and a dramatic ending:

> Climbing up the tree-house one by one
> Climbing up the tree-house one by one
> Falling down the tree trunk, wheeeeee . . . ouch!

Oscar's picture to accompany his song is shown in Figure 2.1.

- Free vocal play in which children explore a wide range of sounds and effects without concern for conventions of story. The musical structure may be complex but unconventional. Davies (1994: 127) describes these as 'the secret songs of children'.

The evidence from the children's songs often shows a musical aware- ness greater than that shown in other activities such as class singing or

Figure 2.1 Oscar's picture to accompany his song.

playing instruments. As Davies (1992: 21) suggests, while children's 'instrumental compositions might show them to be still in the earliest stages . . . the songs of infants, being less "technical", might show a greater degree of development'.

The National Curriculum

Between the ages of 5 and 7, expectations of children's progress are described in the National Curriculum levels (QCA 1999). During Key Stage 1, it is expected that children will be working within levels 1 to 3, and by the end of the stage, most children are expected to have reached level 2. In general terms, this means that they are expected to recognize and explore how sounds can be made, changed and organized. Whereas some children will be able to sing in tune with expression, for most their singing will show a sense of the shape of the melody, though not necessarily reproducing the exact pitches or pitch relationships. When playing instruments, children will be able to play simple patterns and accompaniments, keeping to a steady pulse while performing. In their creative music-making, children will choose sounds carefully in response to a range of stimuli and order them into simple structures such as beginning, middle and end. Some will show an aptitude for combining sounds to create particular effects. Children will respond to different moods in music, with some understanding of how the musical elements can be used to create different moods and effects. They will be able to represent sounds with symbols, and to make improvements to their own work. The descriptions of development and examples that we have outlined above show that all of these competences are being developed from an early age.

Musical literacy

In western culture, considerable emphasis is placed on written music and much music teaching is based on developing children's competence from written to practical forms. The status of written music is such that many competent musicians feel themselves to be unmusical if they cannot read or write music. Gardner (1994) presents as something to be admired that children as young as 2 or 3 can be trained to read music. This flies in the face of what early childhood practitioners believe about learning, which is that understanding grows from the concrete or enactive towards symbolic forms. Moreover, such early training does not of itself lead to musical success.

There is considerable interest (for example, Bamberger 1982; Davidson and Scripp 1986) in trying to stimulate invented notations amongst young children, in order to develop awareness of children's understanding of

Table 2.1 The five symbol systems used by children to record songs

Type	Description
Pictorial	A variety of pictures, icons and images referring to the subject of the song, but carrying no specific musical information
Abstract patterning	Lines and dots which children use to represent the notes of the song and record musical features
Rebus	Alternations of icons, conventional signs and words to depict the text or illustrate the lyrical content and occasionally reveal musical features
Text	Words, letters or imitations of conventional language systems concerned primarily with the text but may be organized to show some musical features
Combination/elaboration	Simultaneous use of abstract symbols and words to represent the text and musical dimensions together

Source: based on Davidson and Scripp 1986: 204–9.

musical structures and conventions. If children's notations are taken as a window on their thinking rather than as simply a preparation for the use of conventional notations, they can offer some very useful insights.

Davidson and Scripp (1986) have used their study to identify characteristics of children's different approaches to written representations of songs. They describe five different symbol systems commonly used by children to record songs (Table 2.1).

Davidson and Scripp (1986: 209) conclude that:

> Children between the ages of five and seven not only change radically in their choice of symbol systems to represent songs, but also show a dramatic increase in the level of sophistication of their notations.

They suggest the developmental sequence shown in Table 2.2 and see the value of these representations as being about the light they throw on children's developing understanding:

> Contained in children's spontaneous notations of short nursery songs are glimpses of growing minds at work. As we better understand children's extraordinary invented symbol systems for music, we discover how they mindfully abstract and reconstruct an increasingly rich and integrated world of musical understanding.

> (1986: 228)

Figure 2.2 Examples of children's notations of the song *Row, Row, Row your Boat*. *Source*: Davidson and Scripp 1986: 205–8.

(a) Emily's (age 6) pictorial system.

(b) Janet's (age 6) abstract patterning system.

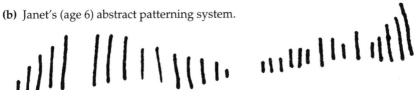

(c) Aaron's (age 6) rebus system.

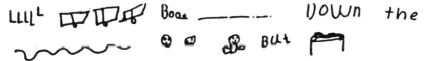

(d) Eleanor's (age 6) text system.

Roa Roa — Roa You'r Boat
chenty. Down the Stream merly merly merly
life is But a dream.

(e) Mary's (age 6) elaboration and combination system.

LA L-LA L-LA   Row, Row, Row Your boat getley

Down the Stream. Merely, merely merly life is but A dream

Table 2.2 Developmental sequence of notation systems used by children to record music

Age	Notation system	Used to describe
5 years	Pictures and abstract symbols	Musical structure or the units of the phrase
6 years	Abstract or language symbols	Underlying pulse, rhythmic grouping or melodic contour
7 years	Language combined with and modified by abstract symbols	Multiple features of the music with particular attention to melodic contour

Source: based on Davidson and Scripp 1986: 209.

Creative development

There are links between musical development and development in the use of other creative media. Music, drawing, imaginative play, dance and block play are some of the many forms of symbolic representation used by children. All of these forms involve play and exploration and their development corresponds to and supports children's ability to express their growing understanding of the world around them. Practitioners who lack confidence in music can use their understanding of other forms of creative development and apply them to music.

Bruner (1982) outlines a staged theory of the development of symbolic representation. This has influenced later theories in describing a movement from early physical or enactive modes of representation through iconic modes, towards increasingly abstract or symbolic forms which can be seen across a range of creative media. Bruner emphasizes that the development of the ability to use the later, symbolic modes does not displace the use of the earlier modes. In music this is particularly clear. Physical engagement with music does not disappear once you can play an instrument or read music. When young children move spontaneously in response to music this is an enactive form of representation. In later, more complex, learning situations, adults may still need to have recourse to physical engagement with music in order to solve particular problems.

More recent theories have attempted to chart children's creative development across different media. Gardner (1993b: 74), for example, has identified four 'waves of development' in relation to symbolic play. Table 2.3 is based on his work and can be applied, Gardner believes, to all aspects of symbolic representation.

Hargreaves and Galton (1992) identify three phases of what they term *artistic development*:

- presymbolic – from birth to 2 years of age;
- figural – from 2 to 5 years of age, involving concrete action;
- schematic, from 5 to 8 years of age, with a focus on realism.

Bannan (2000) is critical of these theories and suggests that in attempting to compare different aspects of creative development, they do not draw sufficiently on what is known about children's music-making: 'things children do are noticeably absent; and what is present . . . fails

Table 2.3 Gardner's four waves of development in symbolic play

Wave	Age	Description	Gardner's examples
1	18 months to 2 years	Event or role structuring	In drawing a truck the child will represent movement and sound but not a graphic equivalent
2	3 years	Topological mapping	In singing a song the child reflects large shifts in pitch direction without detailed accuracy
3	4 years	Digital mapping	Children give great attention to detail, wanting to count everything, e.g. tones in a melody
4	5–7 years	Notational or second-order symbolization	Making marks which themselves refer to a set of marks, e.g. a tally system to keep track of progress in a game

Source: based on Gardner 1993b: 74.

entirely to capture the nature of [child] vocal behaviour' (Bannan 2000: 297).

In addition, in both theories the stages identified are linked to specific ages. Specified ages can never be completely accurate, since children will not achieve the same level in all areas of creative development. Moreover, some children have more experience of some artistic and representational media than others and therefore achieve higher levels.

One of the most important features of children's continuing creative development is play. When children play, they are representing events and exploring materials in order to make better use of their expressive properties. Children's language play contributes to both their linguistic and their musical development. Symbolic play also occurs in drawing or other mark-making, storytelling or imaginative play sequences, the use of three-dimensional materials, and in dance. In Reggio Emilia, a town in northern Italy, children from 0 to 6 years of age are encouraged to explore a wide range of media and materials, translating their ideas from one form of symbolic representation to another. Understanding is enhanced as children find a new perspective on something they have already explored in one art form, by exploring it in a new medium. In using the hundred languages of children, as these symbolic modes are termed (Edwards *et al.* 1993), children achieve high standards of representation, which are based on the same playful and exploratory approaches that characterize language learning. Play and exploration remain important, even when children have reached advanced stages.

While there are many similarities between different areas of creative development, there may also be some differences. Athey (1990) has identified a range of patterns of behaviour which she terms *schemas* and her theory has been influential in practitioners' understanding of the development of symbolic representation. Children's preferred schemas may be found in their drawings (Matthews 1994), in their block play (Gura 1992) and in other forms of imaginative play (Bruce 1987). However, although we can see these patterns of behaviour in dance and in the way children use musical instruments, they are more difficult to detect in children's singing and compositions. This may be because schemas are essentially a way of using space, whereas music is a time-based art form.

Gifted and talented

In Chapter 1 the idea that everyone is born musical was discussed in detail. However, as with all areas of development, some children show earlier signs of greater ability than others. While it remains important to cater for the needs of all children, it is also important that those who show particular aptitude or ability are enabled to develop their potential. QCA (2001a) has published curriculum guidelines for identifying and supporting musically talented children. While these are designed for work with older children, the indicators they put forward may help adults to recognize musical talent in younger children. The guidelines suggest that a child with musical talent:

- is captivated by sound and engages fully with music;
- selects an instrument with care and then is unwilling to relinquish the instrument;
- finds it difficult not to respond physically when hearing music;
- memorizes music quickly without any apparent effort;
- sings and plays music with a natural awareness of the musical phrase – the music makes sense;
- demonstrates the ability to communicate through music, for example to sing with musical expression and with confidence;
- shows strong preferences, single-mindedness and a sustained inner drive to make music.

(QCA 2001a)

When working with very young children, practitioners may or may not consider it desirable or helpful to focus intently on any one area of development. There is a danger that supporting a single interest may narrow the child's opportunities to learn and explore across the curriculum. A 4-year-old who shows particular musical ability remains a 4-year-old with the full range of developmental needs shown by any other child of the same age. Some children with precocious musical talents are channelled into a rather narrow lifestyle which, while undoubtedly supporting their musical talent, may prevent them from developing other important interests. However, it is still important to offer the environment and provision which will allow children to develop their interests and abilities at a high level. In doing so the musical development of all children will be supported. As Kendall (1986: 38) reminds us:

> To label a child as 'scientific', 'musical', 'athletic', and then to concentrate his/her efforts and learning exclusively in that one area is to encourage many other powers to atrophy: aptitudes and preferences

are real, but respecting them does not demand the neglect of less dominant powers.

Conclusion

In this chapter we have looked at patterns of children's musical development. We have also seen how these patterns can be strongly influenced by the environment and culture, particularly at an early age. This means that although we are all born musical, our musical development can take many different forms. If we do not live in a musical environment or receive enough musical stimulation, our musical development may be limited as a consequence. In the chapters that follow we look first at the music curriculum and then at how music can support other aspects of learning, both at home and within a group setting. In the final part we go on to consider how to create a positive environment for 'musicking'.

Part 2

Music in education

The music curriculum

Music has long been an integral part of early childhood education. In the first half of the nineteenth century, Robert Owen emphasized its importance in the nursery at New Lanark, the country's first workplace nursery. Music and dancing were important in Owen's own family life and he gave them a firm place in the early childhood curriculum (Donnachie 2000). Froebel identified singing between mothers and babies as a vital element in the young child's education and saw music as 'one of the prime means by which happiness could be engendered and expressed' (Lilley 1967, cited by Kendall 1986: 45).

Throughout the first half of the twentieth century, music and accompanying movement were characteristic activities of nurseries. Although many individual practitioners believe that music is important, more recently it has had a lower profile in the care and education of young children. This may be because fewer adults perceive themselves as having the necessary skills. It may also be because there have been other pressures in the curriculum, particularly with an increased emphasis on literacy and numeracy. The availability of recorded music may also have influenced this decline. Adults may find recordings easier to use than live music and may compare themselves unfavourably with the quality of the recorded performance.

Nevertheless, current developmental research underlines the importance of music in the lives of young children. Its impact on and relationship with the development of emotion, communication and playfulness make it an invaluable part of the curriculum. In this chapter we consider

Percussion group, c. 1900.

music in its own right as an important element in the education of all children.

Music as a language

Music is a vehicle for expression and communication. All human beings are born with the capacity to make music. Music therefore has many of the features of language and can be approached in a similar way. This was recognized by Her Majesty's Inspectorate of Schools (HMI) when it stated that:

> Learning music has something in common with the acquisition of language. The early stages are largely intuitive, depending on the ear and involving a great deal of memorising, imitation and experimentation.
>
> (HMI 1985: 1)

This link is also recognized by many musicians, who often talk about musical communication in terms that are reminiscent of verbal language. Like verbal language, music exists in several forms. Table 3.1 gives a comparison.

Table 3.1 Comparison of verbal language and music

Verbal language	Music
Unprepared speaking, e.g. normal conversation	Unprepared singing/playing, e.g. improvisation
Prepared speaking from an outline, e.g. a lesson/session plan	Improvisation around a structure, e.g. chord pattern
Speaking from a script, e.g. prepared speeches, acting	Prepared performance, e.g. concert
Listening	Listening
Responding, e.g. a conversation	Group improvisation, where players 'feed off' each other
Written words, e.g. letters, memos	Handwritten manuscript or any form of devised graphic score
Printed words, e.g. books, newspapers	Sheet music

Source: Harrison and Pound 1992: section 2.

In referring to improvisation, we are using the term to mean making up any kind of music spontaneously, drawing on any level of prior experience and knowledge of music-making. The parallel between talk and musical improvisation is particularly significant:

> Both can be direct and unscripted expressions of each individual's unique feelings, emotions and ideas. Both draw on and adapt a vocabulary which has been acquired from a range of sources, including exploration and the talk or improvisation of others. Both can be undertaken alone or in dialogue and dialogues are most successful when participants take account of others' contributions.
>
> (Harrison and Pound 1996: 237)

Improvisation: the 'talk' of music

In learning a language, considerable experience of speaking and listening precedes reading and writing. Similarly in music, considerable experience of exploring, improvising and listening should precede working with written forms.

Learning to talk involves playful interactions between adults and children in which adults:

- value and take pride in the baby's vocal play;
- attempt to make sense of the baby's vocalizations;
- build on the sounds the baby makes and play about with them, changing pitch, tempo, dynamics;
- place an emphasis on communication and not on getting it right.

If we are treating music as a language, then all these characteristics should be present in the teaching and learning of music. The role of play in a developmental process such as music or language learning cannot be overestimated. This is reflected in the fact that we describe ourselves as 'playing' music.

The six principles set out below were developed as part of a music education project with children of school age (Harrison and Pound 1996: 237–8), but are equally relevant for younger children. They are derived from what is known about the development of language.

1 *All children are musical and able to express themselves through music*
We have seen in Chapters 1 and 2 how the ability to make music is an essential human attribute, and that music serves a range of important functions in all human societies. We have also recognized the fundamental importance of music to children's early development. From birth, the use of musical elements by adults and infants supports the expression of feelings and paves the way for all later communication.

2 *Exploration and enjoyment are central to the learning process*
We have also seen that playfulness is both a function and an outcome of music-making. Fun and playfulness were characteristics of the early experience of the musicians studied in the researches of Sloboda and Davidson (1996) and Sosniak (1985). Many other musicians testify how an extended period of free exploration enabled them to take on the discipline of more formal learning at a later stage.

3 *Music learning is a developmental process*
In common with other developmental processes like talking and drawing, the more you do the better you get. Children are more likely to give large amounts of time to an activity that they find pleasurable. The amount of time available in adult-directed musical activities is too short for children to develop expertise. This means that the organization of the music curriculum should ensure that children have more open access to opportunities for musical play and exploration, in order to learn for themselves. We should remember that play is practice but not all practice is play.

4 *Adults can use what they know about supporting the development of language to support children's musical development*
Everyone who lives and works with young children has expertise in the

field of language development. When music is approached as a language, even those who feel they have no musical expertise can adapt familiar strategies to support musical rather than verbal language.

5 *Children learn most effectively when they understand the purpose of what they are doing and can relate it back to their own experience*

This is true of all learning and particularly true in relation to young children. It is a central tenet of early childhood education that we must work from the child's interest and enthusiasm, and this is equally true of their musical development. Practitioners and carers will need to use their observations and knowledge of what children can do and enjoy in deciding future activities and learning experiences.

6 *Children should be offered a range of models which can support and extend their understanding of music*

Children will learn music best in a musically active environment. Just as children who come from families where reading is important read well, so children whose families engage in music are more likely to become involved in music-making. In our society it is the case that many families do not make music with their children. While they may enjoy recorded music, this does not give children the same involvement or understanding of making music. At home and in a group setting, adults may need to offer a wide range of live music opportunities (this is developed further in Chapter 5). It is more important that children see familiar adults making music than that they see expert musicians. The range of role models should also reflect stylistic and cultural diversity.

Aspects of the curriculum

In order to support children's musical development at home or in a group setting, a music curriculum for the early years will need to include the aspects listed below. However, children's music-making cannot be compartmentalized, and adults living and working with young children should recognize how these aspects are interrelated and plan accordingly.

A music curriculum for young children should include:

- singing;
- playing a range of instruments and sound-making materials;
- making up songs in response to a range of stimuli;
- making up music in response to a range of stimuli;
- making up music in response to dance;
- listening to a range of live music;
- listening to a range of recorded music;
- moving in response to music;

- responding to music through the use of a range of creative media, including spoken language;
- recording musical ideas in a range of forms or media.

The content of the curriculum needs to be related to the guidance for the Foundation Stage and the statutory curriculum at Key Stage 1 where appropriate. Although the following section is organized in ages, these boundaries are inevitably somewhat arbitrary. The planned curriculum will vary according to the prior experience of children and the group organization.

In all of these aspects of the music curriculum, children should have opportunities to work both on their own and with others. Adults will need to include strategies which are child-initiated, adult-responsive and adult-directed. This way of categorizing classroom interactions is similar to that adopted by Fisher (1998) and is explained more fully in Chapter 6. In general, the younger the child the more the balance will be weighted in favour of child-initiated activities and the smaller any groupings should be. In the sections that follow we describe the range of experiences which children of different ages may be engaged in. Some aspects have been grouped together to avoid unnecessary repetition.

Singing

0–3 years
In their first year, babies spend a good deal of time babbling and engaging in musical protoconversations with others. They particularly enjoy songs that have a strong pulse and simple, recognizable musical themes. The variety of songs that are sung to young children around the world have these characteristics. The musical conversations which they engage in (see Chapter 1) include imitation on the part of both the adult and the child. The importance of these exchanges between babies and their parents or carers cannot be overemphasized. For very young children in group settings it is vital that the planned experiences include time for adult–child exchanges of this type.

As they get older, children enjoy group singing and will join in with small sections of familiar songs. Action rhymes, where the physical action reinforces the language, are particularly valuable at this age. Songs with simple choruses and repeated phrases provide memorable and predictable structures which help them to join in. A small group of children under 2 years of age joined in with staff in a variety of ways as favourite songs were sung. One child of 14 months simply swayed back and forth in response to the song. Another, aged 20 months, joined in with the actions. Two older children were able to combine some words and actions.

3–5 years
Children of this age enjoy repeating familiar songs and they develop a repertoire of favourites. A study by Maclean *et al.* (1987) identified the most popular nursery rhymes of 3-year-olds. These were (not in order of preference): *Humpty Dumpty, Baa-Baa Black Sheep, Hickory Dickory Dock, Jack and Jill went up the Hill* and *Twinkle, Twinkle Little Star*. Songs such as this, with identifiable melodies and repeated words and syllables, remain very suitable for children of this age. At this age the range within which children can sing comfortably remains quite limited (Young and Glover 1998). It is important that they gain confidence singing within this range before they are expected to tackle songs that include a wider melodic compass. There is no need to require young children to sing high notes accurately, although they may enjoy experimenting with their voices. In addition, while recognizing children's need to repeat the familiar, it is important to provide opportunities to learn an ever-increasing range of songs drawn from a variety of sources.

5–7 years
During these years, children can begin to develop a wider repertoire of songs. Throughout this period, their ability to sing in tune continues to develop, at least within their 'natural' vocal range, and most 7-year-olds can at least follow the contours of a melody. Songs chosen should offer opportunities to develop vocal control in other ways, including dynamics and tone quality. A song like *Coming up the Valley*, for example, describes a journey up and down a valley. It provides an opportunity for children to gradually increase the volume of their singing as they approach the end of the valley, and then to let the volume die away as they go off into the distance. Singing a slow call-and-response song, such as *Tongo*, enables children to practise sustaining longer notes, following the example of the adult. Children can also tackle songs which begin to extend their vocal range.

Playing a range of instruments and sound-making materials

0–3 years
Over time, young children come to associate particular sounds with their sources. Opportunities to play with and explore a wide range of household objects, instruments and other materials will enhance their ability to

link sounds with materials. Any materials given to children of this age must of course be safe and hygienic. Purpose-made rattles made from wood and plastic will produce different sounds, as will those with different fillings. Children can become familiar with a range of ways of making sounds – shaking, scraping, banging, blowing, plucking. Many of the materials provided for heuristic play (Goldschmied and Jackson 1994) provide just such opportunities for sound exploration. Ariel, aged 2, used both conventional instruments and toys to explore rhythms. On one day she used a pair of cymbals to create a repeated pattern which involved clashing them together three times in front of her and once above her head. A few days later, she was observed playing with two small plastic horses and, with one in each hand, using them to create a rhythm in time to music that was playing in the nursery.

Goldschmied and Jackson (1994: 139) suggest that high quality instruments should be provided for children of this age, but add that they should be

> used in a planned way, like the objects for heuristic play . . . a small group of children approaching their third year can learn to play different rhythms, choose instruments and, with help from an adult, create a satisfying musical sound . . . What matters, as with all kinds of play, is the child's experience, not any kind of end product or performance.

3–5 years

Children aged 3–5 years will often play for extended periods with collections of sound-making instruments. The curriculum therefore should be concerned with encouraging them to develop increasing levels of control within musical contexts, such as echoing rhythms played by an adult, or accompanying a song. They are often interested in imitating sounds in the environment and this may be a feature of story sessions where they use instruments to represent features in the story. Large group sessions can be used to establish musical conventions such as conducting, with both adults and children taking turns in this role. These sessions can also enable children to explore concepts such as dynamics and texture. A group of 3- and 4-year-olds explored some percussion instruments with their teacher in order to accompany their singing. They became interested in making the same instrument sound either loud or quiet, to reflect the dynamics of the songs. They were also interested in trying to imitate sounds referred to in the songs. Children described some sounds as being like bells, or like the horn on the bus.

All too often, children are allowed to explore quiet modes of music-making but loud music-making is less often encouraged. In Chapter 5 we consider how outdoor music-making offers opportunities to play loudly. This experience enables children to explore the communicative and expressive potential of dynamics and the physical sensation of playing loudly, without which they may be more reluctant to control their playing at a later stage. As well as using conventional and unconventional instruments, children's increasing coordination makes the use of body sounds (clapping, clicking, stamping) a possibility as an additional part of their repertoire. Physical activities such as this help to develop a secure sense of rhythm. Two 4-year-old boys in an early years centre enjoyed making shakers from junk materials. Once finished to their satisfaction, they began shaking them and dancing excitedly as they made the sounds. At another nursery school, one of the adults had established a focused group activity on making shakers. These were very popular with the children, who became animated and used them at every available opportunity. They took them outside and played them as they rode around the garden on wheeled toys. They took them to a singing session and used them to accompany the songs. In both these examples, children's 'ecstatic response' (Egan 1991: 124) is contributing to their development by shaping the chemistry of the brain and supporting memory, creating optimum conditions for learning (Eliot 1999; Siegel 1999).

5–7 years
Children of this age will be able to handle a wider range of instruments in a more controlled way, with an increased understanding of pulse and pitch. Classroom activities may include a broader range of group activities, developing more complex forms of conducting and accompaniment, and may include performing for others. In an infants school, a year 2 class had made their own musical instruments, and had explored making improvised music together with children as conductors. They were keen to share their music-making and the teacher allowed them to play as other children came in to the whole school assembly. One child was chosen as conductor and signalled different groups of players to start or stop playing at different times. The performance was characterized by high levels of confidence and concentration among all the players, and a high level of interest from the children in the audience.

Activities using untuned percussion instruments develop their growing ability to play in time with others. As the understanding of pitch develops, children will be able to explore the potential of tuned instruments, for instance by trying to work out familiar tunes by ear. Interest in doing this is often sparked by the chance discovery, during exploratory play, that they have played the first few notes of a known tune. This has a parallel in children's drawings. Wales (1990: 143, citing Franklin 1973):

> Initially . . . 'the child stumbles into symbolisation with little or no intention'. He makes a pattern and sees it as a representation, apprehending some correspondence between the pattern and a known object. This is followed by a shift toward deliberate preplanned symbolisation.

Some children may be beginning specialized tuition on an instrument such as the piano, recorder or violin. It is important that these experiences and skills can be brought into the classroom so that children can apply them in different situations and make links between different kinds of music learning. Adults should also recognize the benefits of a broader focus in relation to instrumental learning. Davidson (1994: 128) writes: 'a developmental perspective suggests that a range of musical instruments and contexts be explored rather than a restrictive focus of musical study and instruction on an instrument of choice'.

Making up songs in response to a range of stimuli

Making up music in response to a range of stimuli

Making up music in response to dance

0–3 years
Children's early explorations with their voices lay the foundation for the song creation which develops throughout the pre-school years. If adults recognize and value the imaginative properties demonstrated in children's earliest explorations, children are likely to be encouraged to develop confidence in their creative abilities. Three-year-old Mehdi was playing with plastic knights and discovered a tiny harp amongst the accessories. He pretended to pluck the harp and sang his own tune to go with it.

Papousek's (1994) description of the voice as the first toy should remind us to encourage these early vocalizations through imitation and interaction. Adult engagement is the strongest stimulus at this stage. From the second year of life, snatches of known songs are interspersed with improvised sound to produce song-like sequences.

3–5 years
This is where pot-pourri songs develop into long sequences. Children can be encouraged to persevere with and develop such spontaneous songs when adults show interest, perhaps joining in with the child's song or teaching the song to other children. An experience of singing a wide range of known songs will give children models to draw on in their own song creation. As well as structural models, stimuli for songwriting or music-making can be found in stories, word play, pictures or real-life experiences. Children should have opportunities to make spontaneous, improvised music on voice and instruments without the constraints of having to remember it or write it down. Adult-led activities focusing on improvisation may be reflected in children's spontaneous individual or small-group play. Four-year-old Saskia went outside into the garden just as a gust of wind blew. She used her voice and body to look and sound like the wind. Trang, also aged 4, was drawing a butterfly and began to make up a song about it. As she developed the song, she moved her hips from side to side in time with her singing. While playing outside with a telephone, Alexander created a rhythmic message for a nearby adult:

> It's a train, woo, woo
> We got to have tickets, oo oo oo
> Charlie chalk too oo oo
> Got a video oo oo oo

Children may be introduced to the idea of creating music in response to movement through the use of instruments such as ankle bells which require full physical engagement. The benefits of physical activity in relation to music cannot be overstated. As George Odam (1995: 21) says: 'Musical learning is considerably enhanced and reinforced by the application of movement'. Schools and nurseries lucky enough to have access to a soundbeam can similarly reinforce the physical aspects of musical development. A soundbeam is particularly good for children with special educational needs since even small movements can be translated into sound.

5–7 years
Although children's spontaneous song-making has been observed to decline at this stage, we have seen in Chapter 2 that, with appropriate encouragement, children can progress to new levels of creativity. This important aspect of the curriculum should continue to be developed. It often needs little more than encouragement and the provision of a tape-recorder. As with younger children, adults should continue to introduce a

wide range of new songs in a variety of styles and structures which can act as models for children's own songs:

- imitative songs such as *Tongo*;
- leader–chorus songs such as *Train is a Comin'*; *Hill and Gully Rider*;
- four-line songs with repeating elements such as *The Wheels on the Bus*;
- verse-and-chorus songs such as *Tingalayo*;
- repetitive songs such as *Ten in the Bed*;
- cumulative songs such as *I Know an Old Lady*.

Group song-making can help to develop new ideas and can give confidence to the more reticent children. Children's free vocal play (Davies 1994) often does not include words and therefore provides a good link with other kinds of music creation.

Creative music-making on instruments can be promoted through some more structured group activities, such as making music to illustrate stories; making music in response to poetry, pictures or artefacts; creating accompaniments for songs and movement or dancing. Children will increasingly be able to undertake these activities as a form of collaborative groupwork.

Listening to a range of live music

Listening to a range of recorded music

0–3 years
Even though babies and young children respond excitedly to some forms of recorded music, they gain more benefit from and prefer live music. Even if adults lack confidence in their own level of competence, it is likely that the immediacy of their live performance will have more impact than recordings of the most proficient musicians. Singing at regular, frequent intervals, responding to children's spontaneous singing and joining in with their songs are important alongside more planned group singing sessions.

Although live music will have a strong impact, recorded music is still enjoyed by very young children. Where different kinds of music are playing at different times of day, 1- and 2-year-olds will often move in a variety of ways in response to the music. Shianna rocked herself backwards and forwards, moved her legs and swung herself halfway round. Georgia, on the other hand, danced with her upper body to the music while sitting in the sand tray. One-year-old Tomas moved from side to side, shaking his head, clapping his hands and smiling in recognition of familiar music.

3–5 years

Live music remains important, but recorded music can play a growing part in children's listening. However, children of this age will need help to get full benefit from listening to it. Recordings of familiar songs are popular. When selecting recordings, it is worth remembering that during this period children are just beginning to recognize familiar song tunes when played without the words, and some instrumental recordings of these tunes alongside the sung versions may help them to make the relevant connections.

It may be helpful to develop collections of short pieces that are linked in some way – for example, collections of counting songs or lullabies from different cultures; collections of music played on similar instruments. Children's listening can be helped if there are pictures that relate to the music. One of the disadvantages of recorded music is that children are unable to see how the sounds are produced. Video clips of musicians and singers – again short and with a clear focus – may give children information that sound recordings lack. An opportunity to see and perhaps handle an instrument which features in a piece of recorded music may also help children to make links between what they hear and what they see.

In listening to live music, children should have the opportunity to join in and should certainly be encouraged to move, since the physical movement will enhance their listening and understanding.

5–7 years

By this stage, children are more able to recognize tunes with or without the words, and this means that recordings may include a wider range of music. As concentration develops, longer pieces can also be played. A library of short recorded pieces from which children themselves can select may include tapes with a theme (e.g. instruments, styles, cultural function). The library may include tapes of children's own performances and compositions. The music area should therefore include or give access to a tape-recorder. Pictures, videos and visual images continue to support children's knowledge and understanding of the context in which the music is played.

Live music should continue, but at this age children often enjoy performing to one another. Time and space can be provided for them to do this. One nursery school has an outside performance area which children use as part of their play activity.

Outdoor performance area.

Responding to music through the use of a range of creative media, including spoken language

Recording musical ideas in a range of forms or media

0–3 years
Even before birth, babies move in response to musical stimuli and this process continues throughout infancy. Enjoyment of music is often signalled by expressive movement. Parents and practitioners encourage this in their day-to-day contact with babies by moving around the room in time to music while holding the baby; enabling the baby to bounce in time to the music while standing on their laps; and moving arms and legs in time to music while changing or dressing the baby. As motor control increases, a wider range of dancing movements is used and this should be encouraged by the provision of different kinds of music to dance to. Live music is especially stimulating and may be provided through singing as well as the use of instruments.

Adults should make use of a wide vocabulary in describing music and sounds as this will provide the basis for children's evaluation or appraisal of music at a later stage. At this stage, much of children's response to music is implicit and it may be difficult to get such young children to draw or paint their responses to music. However, if music is playing or going on while children are engaged in activities such as drawing or painting, it is likely that what they produce will be influenced by the sounds they are hearing. This can be a preparation for more conscious artistic responses to musical stimuli at a later age.

3–5 years

For children of this age, physical movement continues to be their most important form of response. As Odam (1995: 21) reminds us: 'Moving to music is natural and an important part of our early and later learning process . . . there is nothing that you can hear in music that cannot somehow be expressed in movement.' Glover (2000: 42) reinforces this view:

> The deep-rooted connection between moving and 'sounding' is of prime importance as a source of young children's musical expression. These parallel modes of time-based activity seem to be intrinsically connected.

Three- and four-year-olds as a whole class group were gathering on the carpet before story time, while Beethoven's *Pastoral Symphony* was playing in the background. The children began to wave their arms in time to the music and this physical movement sustained their interest and their ability to listen for several minutes. Later in the week, a group from the same class were playing in the home corner. Some rock music was playing on the CD player and the teacher reported that the children 'really boogied to the music'.

Opportunities for dancing or expressive movement to music should continue to be encouraged. As discussed in Chapter 2, even at this age, boys may need specific encouragement and stimuli to ensure that they maintain involvement.

The language input made by adults to heighten children's awareness of features of music plays an increasingly important role. Practitioners may develop some structured activities to encourage children to make graphic or pictorial responses to music. Work observed in Reggio Emilia involved encouraging children to link sounds on a metallophone to strips of colour taken from a colour chart and promoted wide-ranging discussion about sound qualities. More conventional activity, but still of equal value, involves asking children to paint their responses to a piece of recorded music.

5–7 *years*

By this stage, children's response to music may often be verbal. This response can be encouraged by some structured activities such as talking about music; comparing two pieces of music or two versions of the same song; discussing the feelings evoked by particular instruments or melodies. Postcards or other visual images can be used to stimulate discussion. A teacher played a piece of music to a small group of children who had in front of them a collection of ten postcards showing very varied images. The set included a seascape, an abstract painting, Van Gogh's *Sunflowers*, a picture of a train and a photograph of a sculpture. Children were asked to say which of the images the music could describe and why. Those who found discussion difficult were helped by the visual images as they provided a starting point for exchanging ideas and preferences.

Older children may also like to write about music, describing either what they hear, the feelings they think it expresses, or what it makes them think about. These written responses could take the form of poetry or creative writing and may be developed collaboratively.

However, increased competence in spoken and written language should not mean that other forms of response, including through dance, movement, drawing and painting, are allowed to decline. They should remain as important mechanisms of expression as they develop parts of the brain and ways of thinking not developed through spoken or written language. The approach of practitioners in Reggio Emilia to symbolic representation underlines the value of representation in a variety of media. In translating ideas from one medium to another, the child is enabled to rethink their understanding.

Another form of representation of musical ideas is notation. For many adults, notation simply means standard western notation, but in fact there are many ways of recording music in written or graphic forms and these may serve different functions. As children grow older, their interest in improvisation may develop into a desire to return to the same musical ideas and create a composition. At this stage, opportunities to invent ways of recording their ideas will be helpful. Some children, for instance those who are learning to play an instrument, may draw on the model of standard notation, but we can also offer other models for them to consider. A range of such models is provided in *Let's Compose* (Harrison 2001). The approaches outlined in Chapter 2 of this book may serve as a basis for supporting children who are at a stage of wishing to preserve their ideas in this way. At this stage, notation is better used as a means of recording than as a tool for learning how to play specific tunes. While some writers (Pugh and Pugh 1998) favour an early introduction to conventional western notation, others contest this view. As Odam (1995: 46) says:

In the primary phase before eleven it is important for teachers to concentrate on building up first the musical equivalent of expressive speech – singing, improvising, playing – and regularly and naturally using the materials of music. Until children are fluent in these behaviours it is completely unnecessary and probably harmful to encourage them to write anything down using formal systems. Just as you need to talk before you write, so natural musical expression must be firmly established first. Children only need to write something when they know what it is they wish to write and have it firmly in their memories.

The statutory curriculum

Table 3.2 shows how the aspects of the curriculum we have identified above relate to the *Curriculum Guidance for the Foundation Stage* (QCA 2000) and the National Curriculum programmes of study for Key Stage 1 (QCA 1999).

The *Curriculum Guidance for the Foundation Stage* does not divide the music curriculum into different areas of activity. However, the stepping stones and early learning goals for music do correspond to the aspects outlined above. In addition, there is specific reference to music in other sections of the guidance – for instance, elsewhere in the creative development section, and in the section on language and communication – which we have referred to in Table 3.2. In the remaining areas of learning, musical development is implicit but has not been highlighted in the table.

The programme of study at Key Stage 1 is divided into four main areas:

- Controlling sounds through singing and playing – performing skills. This includes the aspects we have defined which relate to singing and playing instruments alone and with others.
- Creating and developing musical ideas – composing skills. This includes the aspects relating to making up music.
- Responding and reviewing – appraising skills. This includes the aspects relating to responding to music.
- Listening and applying knowledge and understanding. These skills and understandings are intended to underpin the other areas of the Key Stage 1 curriculum. We have therefore included several references to them within Table 3.2 to show how they support, and are developed by, other activities.

An integrated approach is recommended. The National Curriculum programmes of study (QCA 1999) advise that listening and applying knowledge and understanding should be developed through the interrelated skills of performing, composing and appraising.

Table 3.2 Relationships between aspects of the music curriculum and the Foundation Stage and National Curriculum Key Stage 1

Aspects of the curriculum	Foundation Stage	National Curriculum Key Stage 1
Singing	• Join in favourite songs (CD2) • Enjoy joining in with ring games (CD2) • Sing a few simple, familiar songs (CD2) • Begin to build a repertoire of songs (CD2) • Recognize and explore how sounds can be changed (CD2) • Sing simple songs from memory (CD2) • Enjoy joining in with number rhymes and songs (MD)	• Use their voices expressively by singing songs and speaking chants and rhymes (1a) • Listen with concentration (4a) • Internalize and recall sounds with increasing aural memory (4a) • Rehearse and perform with others (1c) • Make improvements to their own work (3b)
Playing a range of instruments and sound-making materials	• Tap out simple repeated rhythms and make some up (CD2) • Explore and learn how sounds can be changed (CD2) • Explore the different sounds of instruments (CD2) • Recognize and explore how sounds can be changed (CD2)	• Play tuned and untuned instruments (1b) • Listen with concentration (4a) • Internalize and recall sounds with increasing aural memory (4a) • Rehearse and perform with others (1c) • Make improvements to their own work (3b)
Making up songs in response to a range of stimuli	• Sing to themselves and make up simple songs (CD2) • Begin to build a repertoire of songs (CD2) • Recognize and explore how sounds can be changed (CD2) • Sing simple songs from memory (CD2)	• Create musical patterns (2a) • Explore, choose and organize sounds and musical ideas (2b) • Understand how the combined musical elements can be organized and used expressively within simple structures (4b)

Aspects of the curriculum	Foundation Stage	National Curriculum Key Stage 1
	• Use their imagination in . . . music (CD3) • Express and communicate their ideas, thoughts and feelings (through) a variety of songs and musical instruments (CD4) • Listen with enjoyment, and respond to stories, songs and other music, rhymes and poems and make up their own stories, songs, rhymes and poems (CLL)	• Make improvements to their own work (3b) • Understand how music is used for particular purposes (4d)
Making up music in response to a range of stimuli	• Tap out simple repeated rhythms and make some up (CD2) • Explore and learn how sounds can be changed (CD2) • Explore the different sounds of instruments (CD2) • Recognize and explore how sounds can be changed (CD2) • Use their imagination in . . . music (CD3) • Express and communicate their ideas, thoughts and feelings through a variety of songs and musical instruments (CD4) • Try to capture experiences and responses with music (CD4)	• Create musical patterns (2a) • Explore, choose and organize sounds and musical ideas (2b) • Understand how the combined musical elements can be organized and used expressively within simple structures (4b) • Make improvements to their own work (3b) • Understand how music is used for particular purposes (4d)

Table 3.2 Continued

Aspects of the curriculum	Foundation Stage	National Curriculum Key Stage 1
Making up music in response to dance	• Use their imagination in . . . music (CD3) • Express and communicate their ideas, thoughts and feelings through a variety of songs and musical instruments (CD4)	• Create musical patterns (2a) • Explore, choose and organize sounds and musical ideas (2b) • Understand how the combined musical elements can be organized and used expressively within simple structures (4b) • Make improvements to their own work (3b) • Understand how music is used for particular purposes (4d)
Listening to a range of live music	• Show an interest in the way musical instruments sound (CD2) • Recognize repeated sounds and sound patterns (CD2) • Listen to favourite nursery rhymes, stories and songs (CLL) • Join in with repeated refrains, anticipating key events and important phrases (CLL)	• Listen with concentration (4a) • Internalize and recall sounds with increasing aural memory (4a) • Understand how the combined musical elements can be organized and used expressively within simple structures (4b) • Understand how sounds can be made in different ways (4c) • Understand how music is used for particular purposes (4d)
Listening to a range of recorded music	• Recognize repeated sound and sound patterns (CD2)	• Listen with concentration (4a) • Internalize and recall sounds with increasing aural memory (4a)

Aspects of the curriculum	Foundation Stage	National Curriculum Key Stage 1
		• Understand how the combined musical elements can be organized and used expressively within simple structures (4b) • Understand how sounds can be made in different ways (4c) • Understand how music is used for particular purposes (4d)
Moving in response to music	• Respond to sound with body movement (CD2) • Enjoy joining in with dancing and ring games (CD2) • Imitate and create movement in response to music (CD2) • Begin to move rhythmically (CD2) • Match movements to music (CD2) • Use their imagination in . . . music and dance (CD3) • Respond to rhythm, music and story by means of gesture and movement (PD)	• Explore and express their ideas and feelings about music using movement and dance (3a) • Understand how the combined musical elements can be organized and used expressively within simple structures (4b) • Understand how music is used for particular purposes (4d)

Table 3.2 Continued

Aspects of the curriculum	Foundation Stage	National Curriculum Key Stage 1
Responding to music through the use of a range of creative media, including spoken language	• Listen with enjoyment, and respond to stories, songs and other music, rhymes and poems and make up their own stories, songs, rhymes and poems (CLL)	• Explore and express their ideas and feelings about music using movement and dance (3a) • Understand how the combined musical elements can be organized and used expressively within simple structures (4b) • Understand how music is used for particular purposes (4d)
Recording musical ideas in a range of forms or media	• Draw and paint, sometimes giving meanings to marks (CLL) • Ascribe meanings to marks (CLL)	• Understand how sounds can be described using given and invented signs and symbols (4c)

CD2   Creative development: music
CD3   Creative development: use of imagination
CD4   Creative development: responding to experiences and expressing and communicating ideas
CLL   Communication, language and literacy
PD   Physical development
MD   Mathematical development
PSE   Personal, social and emotional development

Evaluating approaches to music education

There are many well-established approaches to music education in early childhood. These approaches have many strengths and are based on firm principles. The Kodaly method, for example, offers a structured approach to the development of musical understanding through singing. The Orff approach uses tuned percussion instruments with an emphasis on the pentatonic (five-note) scale and the development of improvisation. The Dalcroze approach is based around movement, while the Suzuki method draws parallels between language learning and music learning and applies them to instrumental teaching. (In addition, some of the published schemes of work for the primary phase begin with activities designed for 4-year-olds. With the introduction of the Foundation Stage, practitioners should remember that children in the reception class are not subject to the National Curriculum.)

Any scheme or approach that is being considered should be looked at carefully to ensure that it meets the developmental needs of the children you are working with. Table 3.3 lists a set of questions which will help you in the evaluation of any approach to the music curriculum.

Table 3.3 Evaluating approaches to the music curriculum

Question	Comment
Are the principles which underpin this approach consistent with your approach to young children's learning? • Is there an assumption that every child is musical? • Is the material accessible to non-specialist practitioners? • Does it draw on a range of styles and cultures and present a positive image of cultural and linguistic diversity? • Does it avoid stereotypes in relation to ethnicity, gender, ability? • Does the approach advocated in the scheme fit in with the general principles which underpin the curriculum as a whole? • Does it value and foster children's musical creativity?	

Table 3.3 Continued

Question	Comment

Is music being taught musically?
- Are the results and processes musical?
- Is there an emphasis on communication and expression?
- Does it offer children an active role in learning through play, exploration, hypothesizing and trial and error?
- Will children have fun doing the activities?
- Are skills taught in a relevant and meaningful context?
- Are adults able to build on what children already know?

Is music being learnt in a social context?
- Is there an age-appropriate balance between class, group and individual work?
- Does it place sufficient emphasis on music as a social activity?
- Does it enable parents to contribute to their children's musical development?

Is the content of the curriculum broad and relevant?
- Is the content relevant to children's own experience?
- Is there an appropriate emphasis on creative music-making?
- Does it recognize the role of aural skills and aural memory?
- Is the content appropriate to the age range?
- Are the activities sufficiently open-ended to ensure that children can join in at their own level?

Conclusion

In this chapter we have identified aspects of a music curriculum for children from birth to 7 years of age. We have looked at children's development within each aspect. Children's development will be strengthened when similar opportunities for music-making are provided in both home and group settings. We have shown the relationship between these aspects of the music curriculum and the statutory requirements for music in the Foundation Stage and at Key Stage 1, and we have provided guidance for the evaluation of some more formalized approaches. In the next chapter we consider the role of music learning across the curriculum.

Music as a tool for learning

Although music can be identified as a specific area of the curriculum, this does not mean that it has to be taught as a separate subject or activity. In the previous chapters we have focused on music in its own right because adults will need to think of it in this way as an organizing feature of their own work. However, young children's learning is not compartmentalized in this way. At home, music may be easily integrated into the patterns of daily life. In group settings, cross-curricular approaches enable children to make links or connections across different areas of learning and music plays an important part in supporting this process. As well as learning to make music and learning about music, children can learn *through* music. In Egan's (1991) terms, it is a 'tool for thinking'.

Hildebrandt (1998: 68) describes the following uses of music in a typical early years setting, most of which could be equally well found in the home:

- to create a warm, positive atmosphere;
- to help ease transitions (between one activity and another);
- to attract the children's attention and re-engage them in a group focus;
- to help children learn social values and behaviours;
- to help children learn letters, numbers, etc.;
- to celebrate special occasions;
- to celebrate ethnic diversity as well as social solidarity;
- to make connections between music, language, visual arts and other areas of the early childhood curriculum.

Cognitive development

There is widespread interest in the role that music may play in supporting cognitive development. Companies are publishing CDs and claiming that listening to the music on them will enhance your baby's intelligence. Other research studies in Europe and the USA have claimed that:

- children who study music do better at everything else;
- children receiving extra music also did better at maths and languages;
- children listening to 10 minutes of Mozart a day increased their spatial intelligence and improved exam results;
- classes of 5–7-year-olds given special music and arts lessons performed better at maths tests.

For the most part, these studies remain inconclusive. Many were undertaken with older children. Some of the studies indicate that the transfer effects of engagement in music may be only temporary. Hallam (2001: 15) summarizes current understandings of research findings as follows:

- research which claimed that listening to Mozart could improve spatial reasoning has proved difficult to replicate;
- studies of the effects of using the Kodaly method on other skills have had mixed results, although music lessons designed to develop auditory, visual and motor skills have benefited reading skills;
- learning to play a musical instrument has been shown to produce small temporary effects on spatial reasoning but not on other aspects of cognitive functioning . . .;
- taking music was positively related to better performance in other subjects, [but] this does not necessarily mean that it was the cause of it.

She concludes:

From our current level of knowledge it is not possible to draw firm conclusions about the effects of listening to or active involvement in music making on our intellectual skills. The jury remains out.

(Hallam 2001: 16)

Music across the curriculum

Music is such an important part of all human life and clearly has a strong motivating effect on all of us, including children, that using music across the curriculum can only have a positive effect on the quality of education.

In the sections that follow, we have placed a strong emphasis on children's personal, social and emotional development; the development of communication, language and literacy; and creative development. These three areas correspond to the three aspects of human development identified in Chapter 1 and which music most strongly supports, namely emotional development, communication and playfulness. These three aspects support all human behaviour and underpin all future learning. They therefore have a particular importance in the curriculum. Since these three aspects of development feature as areas of learning in the *Curriculum Guidance for the Foundation Stage* (QCA 2000), we have chosen the six areas of learning identified in that document as a way of organizing this chapter.

The *Curriculum Guidance for the Foundation Stage* was not designed with children under 3 years old in mind. Whether at home with parents or carers, or in a group setting, babies and toddlers do not necessarily benefit from experiences organized and compartmentalized in this way. At this age, music is integral to all activity.

Similarly, children at Key Stage 1 are subject to the requirements of the National Curriculum and their curriculum will be differently organized. However, as the *Curriculum Guidance for the Foundation Stage* acknowledges, some children, such as those with special educational needs, may need to continue working towards some or all of the early learning goals when they are in year 1 or year 2.

This chapter focuses on the way in which music supports learning in other areas of the curriculum. It is also true that the development of music is in turn supported by learning in other areas. For example, music can help a child to develop an ability to concentrate, but, conversely, a child who can concentrate will be better able to tackle some aspects of musical learning. Glover (2000: 41) points out that children do not differentiate between musical and non-musical experience and emphasizes the importance of a holistic view:

> If the teacher can create an environment in which music is an integrated part of each day's activities, and in which children can continue to pursue music embedded in everything else, the quality of children's music can be maintained.

Personal, social and emotional development

The social and emotional development of very young children underpins all other learning. Babies who fail to form a secure attachment with at least one significant adult will fail to thrive both physically and intellectually. As we have seen, music plays a vital role in establishing intimacy between babies and their carers. The musical elements in protoconversations, the use of universal tunes in expressing emotion, and the playful musical games played by mothers or other adults and babies are of fundamental importance in infancy.

Music continues to play a vital role in children's personal, social and emotional development throughout the early years. It offers a means of expressing and exploring emotion; it promotes social interaction and collaboration through joining in songs, dance and 'band sessions'; and, since it has such a high motivational power, it promotes concentration, confidence and the development of control. Gardner (1993a) reminds us that musical ability alone is of little value without an accompanying social awareness. Those who live or work with young children, from birth onwards, can and should make use of music as a way of support-ing learning.

In the *Curriculum Guidance for the Foundation Stage*, personal, social and emotional development has been divided into six areas. To these we have added sections on citizenship and on spiritual, moral, social and cultural development.

Dispositions and attitudes

Music has the capacity to act as a calming influence and this quality may be used in work with young children. Children also find music exciting and stimulating, and so activities and experiences which include music support the development of a positive attitude to learning. Dowling (2000) identifies motivation, perseverance, curiosity, creativity, problem-solving and reflection as important dispositions for learning, while Carr (2001) defines taking an interest, being involved, persisting with difficulty or uncertainty, communicating with others and taking responsibility as 'domains of learning dispositions'. It is clear that all of these dispositions and attitudes can be developed through music-making.

Self-confidence and self-esteem

When children's spontaneous music-making or singing is recognized and valued, children's sense of self-worth is enhanced. One of the most common points made about children's involvement in music is that it increases their self-confidence. This is in part because making music draws on so many different aspects of ourselves – physical, cognitive, creative, emotional. Music offers an opportunity to express oneself in a fundamental or elemental way since, as we have suggested in Chapter 1, humans danced and sang before they spoke. Even at the earliest stages of development, performing a song or completing a musical activity generates a great sense of achievement. Hallam (2001) cites research evidence that children of low economic status receiving individual piano lessons have also exhibited increases in self-esteem.

Making relationships

Although, as we have seen, there are many innate strategies for communicating with babies, two-way verbal communication is difficult if not impossible. One of the most significant ways in which babies are drawn into the culture and enabled to make relationships with those close to them is through the use of music. Shared music-making continues to offer opportunities to communicate with and relate to others. Susan Young's (2000) work on musical conversations in a nursery school shows clearly the development of close interactive working between adults and children. Group music-making at any age gives a sense of social cohesion, supporting relationships between peers. Many songs offer opportunities for social interaction, and even children who would have difficulties in other situations can be led by the music to follow rules and conventions. Regular involvement in music enhances the social climate of the classroom with children showing 'increased social cohesion . . . greater self-reliance, better social adjustment and more positive attitudes' (Hallam 2001: 16, citing Spychiger *et al.* 1993 and Hanshumaker 1980).

Behaviour and self-control

Making music with others gives children a reason to take turns, listen to others, plan their own actions in relation to others and act in response to cues given by others. In addition, learning to take your part in group music-making requires considerable self-control. It is hard not to shake your shaker until it is your turn. Children can learn to treat instruments with respect and to understand that lack of self-control can result in damage to shared resources.

Self-care and independence

The playful, improvisatory approach to music recommended in this book demands that children make decisions about their own music-making and the resources they need. They are encouraged to work independently.

Resources should be organized in a way that makes it possible for children to choose what they need and select alternatives as they refine their work. Children can also learn to replace those resources that they are not using so that they are available for others. In the early stages of exploration, this can result in some untidiness, but it is a necessary part of the development of independent learning.

Sense of community

Music is one of the most significant ways in which different communities (families, football teams, nations, youth subcultures, religions) articulate their sense of identity. Making music together enables children to feel part of a cohesive whole. This is seen in primary and secondary schools at assembly time, but is also found at home and in early years settings where particular songs may signal significant parts of the day, such as storytime or mealtime. Music can be used to accompany some of the significant daily routines, such as welcome or goodbye songs or songs sung as part of the ritual of going to bed.

In our culturally diverse society, music can provide an accessible initial insight into different traditions. Shared music-making, using music from different cultural roots (such as celebrating different new year ceremonies through song), can offer children an active experience which enables them both to make links with their own experience and to appreciate and understand difference.

Citizenship

When working with children in the early years the government's emphasis on citizenship may best be understood by thinking about groupwork, collaboration, democracy and giving children a voice. There is considerable interest in finding ways to help young children voice their views. A number of national and charitable organizations are exploring ways of enabling babies and very young children to express preferences and opinions. The Listening to Young Children project has been established through a partnership between Coram Family and the Ragdoll Foundation. Their aim is to help professionals gain an understanding of how to listen to young children. The interest of some groups also extends to children with special educational needs who may have difficulties in communication.

Group music-making offers opportunities for children to engage in a range of social processes: stating preferences in front of others in a way that can be understood; justifying opinions and choices; collaboration to achieve an agreed aim; and negotiation to resolve differences of opinion. These and similar processes are vital elements in children's personal and social development and in their understanding of citizenship.

Spiritual, moral, social and cultural development

These aspects of development are integral to many inspections, and it is clear that music has an important part to play (Stead 1999). Spirituality was considered by many of the pioneers of nursery education, such as the McMillan sisters, to be an important focus for development of young children. Although it is difficult to define, it remains important that children develop a capacity for awe and wonder, and music can be a significant means for achieving this. This is expressed by Stead (1999: 131) as follows:

> Because music is abstract, and because it can mirror so closely our 'feelingful' world, it carries a unique form of meaning for us. It is this meaning which sheds light upon that which animates us, that which makes us human in the fullest sense of the word.

Making music is a fundamental way in which different cultures express their identity. Introducing young children to a range of songs and music from a variety of cultures can help them to value cultural diversity and to see the links between these and their home culture. Singing the same song with words in different languages; singing songs celebrating common events or customs in different ways; or listening to music using different instruments can help children to become aware of and enjoy cultural difference.

The relationships between aspects of the music curriculum and aspects of personal, social and emotional development are summarized in Table 4.1.

Table 4.1 Relationships between aspects of the music curriculum and aspects of personal, social and emotional development

Aspects of the music curriculum	Aspects of personal, social and emotional development					
	Dispositions and attitudes	Self-confidence and self-esteem	Making relationships	Behaviour and self-control	Self-care and independence	Sense of community
Singing	Children are highly motivated to sing Singing enables them to channel enthusiasm and to experience success in doing something they want to do	Physical and emotional engagement in all kinds of singing develops an enhanced sense of self	Interactive game songs Partner songs, question and answer songs or duets Enjoyment of singing with others	Songs involving turn-taking Creating a calming atmosphere by singing	Spontaneous songs Independent singing	Group singing time: singing together a range of familiar songs, creating a sense of belonging
Playing a range of instruments and sound-making materials	Children are highly motivated to play instruments and this enables them to channel enthusiasm and to experience success in doing something they want to do	Physical and emotional engagement in all kinds of music-making develops an enhanced sense of self Playing an instrument successfully generates a high sense of achievement	Paired work on instruments	Songs in which instruments are played only at certain times	Making choices about which instruments to play Playing independently	Playing together, creating a sense of belonging

Table 4.1 Continued

Aspects of the music curriculum	Aspects of personal, social and emotional development					
	Dispositions and attitudes	Self-confidence and self-esteem	Making relationships	Behaviour and self-control	Self-care and independence	Sense of community
Making up songs and music in response to a range of stimuli (including dance)	Problem-solving strategies used to find ways of creating the desired effect	Expressing own feelings, ideas	Group composing – collaboration, negotiation, working together to achieve common goal Respect for the ideas and contributions of others	Concentration, focus and discipline are all necessary to see through the process of composing or song-writing	Selecting the desired resources to make music which achieves the intended effect Being able to express moods, emotions and atmospheres	Sharing ideas Performing own music to others Developing collaboration and respect for others Making up songs and music which express home culture
Listening to a range of live or recorded music	Listening to music develops concentration and curiosity	Self-expectation of being able to listen or to be receptive	Listening to each other	Concentration Stillness	Choosing music that you want to listen to or to reflect mood	Listening all together e.g. in assembly or group times
Responding to music through the use of a range of creative media, including dance and spoken language Recording musical ideas in a range of forms or media	Children are motivated to move to music Problem-solving strategies used to find ways of creating an appropriate response	Expressing own feelings, ideas	Sharing ideas and responses	Changing mode of response to reflect different stimuli	Developing a personal response to music including the expression of emotional responses	Developing group responses to stimuli

seen in the street. Mirrors were used to create a sense of crowd and reflection such as that produced in puddles. Further work was done on puddles: the way they look under different conditions and the way they reflect objects around them. Work in any one of the media used in this project would not on its own have enabled children to reflect in the depth achieved through the focus on different senses and forms of representation. Their ability to examine the changes in sound, people and environment was enhanced by the process of representing the impact of rainfall in different forms.

Common concepts across the arts both reinforce one another and help children to understand them. Discussion supports conceptual thinking as children come to recognize difficult concepts like pattern. The idea of pattern in paintings or drawing, patterns in music or movement will be increasingly refined as they are compared and contrasted with one another. Other examples of common concepts include those of shape, space, structure, texture and colour. All of these can be interpreted across different art forms, and the process of doing so enhances children's understanding of their meaning.

Creativity

> Creativity is not unique to the arts. It is equally fundamental to advances in the sciences, in mathematics, technology, in politics, business and in all areas of everyday life.
>
> (NACCCE 1999: 27)

Although creativity is not unique to the arts, the areas of creative development do make an important contribution to creativity. The right hemisphere of the brain is responsible for imagination, the use of metaphor and representation which are all fundamental to creative development. Much of the curriculum in the UK focuses on areas of learning such as reading and mathematics which primarily engage the left hemisphere of the brain. Neuroscience reinforces what many have long believed, namely that stimulation of both hemispheres is necessary to support learning and cognition. The engagement of both hemispheres enables children to develop cross-lateral thinking and problem-solving skills which can be applied in any area of life. We therefore need to provide children with a curriculum which stimulates both hemispheres of the brain. This means promoting creativity throughout the curriculum, in order that left brain activities such as logic and analysis can be tempered by the right brain activities of imagination and insight. Music makes an important contribution to this process.

The NACCCE (1999) report *All Our Futures* defines four features of creativity which can apply to all areas of human activity:

- using imagination – through play and making unusual connections;
- pursuing purposes – sometimes towards unforeseen objectives;
- being original – expressing ideas and feelings in new ways;
- judging value – reflection, developing critical evaluation.

All these features can be found in music when it is taught in such a way as to promote the expression of feelings, communication and playfulness. Hallam (2001: 58, citing Hanshumaker 1980) reinforces this view when she reports that participation in music 'appears to have a significant positive effect on the development of characteristics of creativity'.

The relationships between aspects of the music curriculum and aspects of creative development are set out in Table 4.3.

Mathematical development

Learning to count is greatly supported by the use of number rhymes and songs. Egan (1991: 226) suggests that:

> The first counting systems were embedded in the activities they helped with, . . . and some echoes of these are to be found in the number rhymes that still exist. The rhythmic base of many of these persists in the tunes that accompany them . . . From this one can elaborate the common foundational constituents of mathematics and music by playing games in which numbers and sounds interact.

The way in which music supports memory is further enhanced when actions using fingers are added, since the part of the brain concerned with counting is also the area which governs the fingers (Ramachandran and Blakeslee 1999). Time spent singing *One, two, three, four, five / Once I caught a fish alive* will be well spent.

Pattern is a fundamental characteristic of both music and mathematics. Learning to recognize and create patterns in music can help children to understand the existence of pattern in mathematics. Repeating patterns can be easily understood in musical games. Ann Montague-Smith (1997) outlines patterns to be found in movement, instrumental music-making and singing and the ways in which they can reinforce mathematical ideas.

Understanding of time can be very difficult for young children, but in music, time is felt. A physical sense of when to join in can be experienced in taking part in a chorus song or an action song. Similarly, ideas of

Table 4.3 Relationships between aspects of the music curriculum and aspects of creative development

Aspects of the curriculum	Aspects of creative development		
	Exploring media and materials	Imagination	Responding to experiences and expressing and communicating ideas
Singing		Singing in role or character imagining situations, e.g. creepy, scary	Songs used to communicate, express ideas and feelings
Playing a range of instruments and sound-making materials	Exploring possibilities of sound-makers and instruments	Imaginative use of instruments to express moods and feelings	Music used to communicate and express ideas and feelings
Making up songs and music in response to a range of stimuli (including dance)	Using different media, e.g. pictures, stories, as stimuli for songs and music	Expressing imaginative ideas through improvisation and composition	Children's own songs and music created in response to stimuli
Listening to a range of live or recorded music	Listening provides experience for response Movement to enhance listening	Pictures in your head	Listening provides experience for response
Responding to music through the use of a range of creative media, including dance and spoken language	Multi-media responses – drawing, painting, dance, discussion, etc.	Developing ideas from exploration and describing ideas prompted by music	Responding to music listening (songs and instruments) in a variety of ways
Recording musical ideas in a range of forms or media			

doubling and halving frequently feature in musical activities such as rhythm games. A musical pulse is a form of measuring time. Musical rhythms may be required to fit into lengths of time which are expressed in numbers of beats. Even though the underlying concept of time remains implicit, these activities will contribute to an overall understanding of time.

Structure and symmetry are also common to both music and mathematics and can reinforce one another. As well as linking to conceptual development there is a strong link with pattern. The work of Coral Davies (1992) shows that children may often instinctively improvise songs in a four line structure, even though they would not be able to express the structure explicitly. Music that children compose or improvise may have a structure that has parallels with ideas of symmetry in mathematics.

Positional language is an important part of mathematics for young children. The link between the meaning of words like high and low in mathematical terms and in musical terms is not easily apparent to young children. Some work (Durkin and Townsend 1997) has been undertaken using instruments where high notes are physically higher than low notes in order to reinforce the link between mathematical and musical ideas of high and low. It is possible to buy instruments, such as step glockenspiels or chime bars, or the Vietnamese t'rung hong, on which notes are ordered from low to high with the lowest notes at the bottom and the highest at the top.

Differences in size can be linked to differences in pitch. The Greek mathematician Pythagoras is credited with the discovery of the numerical ratios corresponding to musical intervals (for instance two notes an octave apart have the ratio of 2:1). Instruments like xylophones or Boomwhackers are helpful in illustrating the way in which different lengths of piping or cardboard tubing can produce different sounds. Exploration and discussion of these instruments can help children's understanding in both mathematics and music. They may recognize smaller objects by their higher notes, or lower notes by their larger size.

The relationships between aspects of the music curriculum and aspects of mathematical development are set out in Table 4.4.

Table 4.4 Relationships between aspects of the music curriculum and aspects of mathematical development

Aspects of the curriculum	Aspects of mathematical development		
	Numbers as labels and for counting	Calculating	Shape, space and measures
Singing	Number songs	Counting beats	Comparative language Song structures Beats as measures Notations
Playing a range of instruments and sound-making materials	Counting beats	Jumps and sounds, syllables Playing something twice	Different note sizes on tuned percussion and wind instruments Different amounts of liquid in bottles
Making up songs and music in response to a range of stimuli (including dance)	Making up counting songs with actions	Fitting improvisations into the gaps in music Making up repeated patterns	Making up songs and compositions about shape, space and measures Use of known musical structures creating scores
Listening to a range of live or recorded music	Listening to counting songs How many instruments are playing?	Identifying repeated patterns in music	Listening for structure, duration, tempo, dynamics
Responding to music through the use of a range of creative media, including dance and spoken language	Planning and performing actions and dance steps Describing mathematical aspects of music	Planning and performing actions and dance steps Describing mathematical aspects of music	Identifying and talking about: long and short fast and slow high and low
Recording musical ideas in a range of forms or media			Creating or studying musical scores

Physical development

> Nobody should have to sit still when there's music. It moves, and it makes you move.
>
> (A child quoted in Campbell 1998: 206)

Music and physical development are intricately connected and at no time more so than in the early years. Young and Glover (1998: 36) recognize this:

> Music and movement are inseparable. We physically sense the movement in music and 'hear' the music silently made by movement. The qualities of timing, rhythmic patterning, phrasing and intensity are shared by both. So it makes sense to work with children in music and movement together both in musical terms and in terms of children's learning.

Gardner (1994: 190) describes music in the early years as 'primarily a kinaesthetic experience for the young child'. Odam (1995: 13) agrees that 'much early music education is inseparable from movement education'. Campbell (1998: 198) describes movement as 'a means of knowing music'. She writes:

> Music is more than an auditory sensation: it is a thoroughly and all encompassing physical experience. Children tend to feel music in a visceral way and are compelled to respond to it kinaesthetically. We may strive to provide them with chances to 'listen with their bodies' to music, to dance and move to music in the ways that they find naturally appealing.

Without movement, children's understanding of rhythm may not fully develop or become secure. It is impossible to make music without moving, and this is particularly true of rhythm and pulse.

Moving in response to music can also help children to develop gross motor control. Music may act as a stimulus for movement where children might otherwise be reluctant to engage in physical activity, offering an expressive framework which may be more attractive than exercise for its own sake. Ring games, such as 'There was a princess long ago', offer group support for children who lack the confidence to create their own movements but also help children to coordinate their movements with others.

Fine motor control will be supported by both finger rhymes and action songs and the use of instruments. Children have to find ways to hold an instrument comfortably and effectively. In order to engage in group music-making they must also learn to plan their actions to fit in with those of others in creating an agreed effect. Even more precise control is needed as children become involved in work on rhythm and pulse, or when they need to find specific notes on a tuned instrument. Activities such as drumming or playing a keyboard require the coordinated but different use of both hands, while other musical action games demand coordinated action involving hands, feet and voice.

The relationships between aspects of the music curriculum and aspects of physical development are set out in Table 4.5.

Knowledge and understanding of the world

Musical activity and exploration can support scientific investigation. Looking for similarities and differences in the way sounds can be made, for example, can contribute to conceptual development. Children can categorize objects or instruments according to whether they are blown, struck, scraped or plucked. They can learn about the different properties of a range of materials by comparing the sounds they can make.

Making instruments, in itself a design and technology activity, can help children to understand how sounds are made by conventional instruments. A rainstick is made in South America by pushing thorns into a hollow stick. The thorns obstruct the passage of seeds through the tube giving it the characteristic trickling sound. Clear plastic rainsticks can be purchased which allow children to see what is happening. If children are also helped to make an instrument of this sort they begin to get a clear idea of how the sound is produced.

Music-making, both performing and listening, offers a context for using tape-recorders, CD players and microphones. As well as listening to commercially recorded music, some children may enjoy recording their own songs and music to play for others or to help them evaluate their work. A number of software programs have been designed to support young children's music learning through information and communication technology (ICT). Installations such as a soundbeam or sound-sensitive mats enable children to explore making different sounds by varying their movements. These may be of particular benefit to children whose movement is impaired since even very small movements will make changes in the sounds produced.

Table 4.5 Relationships between aspects of the music curriculum and aspects of physical development

	Aspects of physical development				
Aspects of the curriculum	*Movement*	*Sense of space*	*Health and bodily awareness*	*Using equipment, tools and materials*
Singing	Use of voice in different ways	Singing in different spaces Communicating over different distances	Breathing and posture Songs about the body	
Playing a range of instruments and sound-making materials	Coordinated movement and fine motor control	Turn-taking, negotiating space when playing in a group	Instrument hygiene Body percussion	Range of instruments and sound-makers Using both one and two hands
Making up songs and music in response to a range of stimuli (including dance)	Dance as a stimulus		Songs about hygiene and the body	Range of instruments and sound-makers Using both one and two hands
Listening to a range of live or recorded music		Music performed in different venues, e.g. outdoor, hall, classroom	How the ear works	Tape-recorders, etc.
Responding to music through the use of a range of creative media, including dance and spoken language	Expressive movement and dance	Effective use of available space Awareness of others in group	Proprioception – awareness of body space	Tools and media, e.g. paint brushes, clay, fabric, etc.
Recording musical ideas in a range of forms or media				

Children working with soundbeam.

Music is a way of exploring other times and places, as well as other cultures and beliefs. Sharing favourite pieces of music from home and comparing their own favourite music with that of their parents and grand-parents can start to generate an understanding of differences or similarities in styles, functions and contexts. Inviting musicians into the school or nursery to play different kinds of music can help to broaden children's horizons. Music plays an integral part in children's contact with the practices of different religions and traditions. They can listen to or take part in, for example, lullabies or playground songs from different parts of the world.

The relationships between aspects of the music curriculum and aspects of knowledge and understanding of the world are set out in Table 4.6.

Table 4.6 Relationships between aspects of the music curriculum and aspects of knowledge and understanding of the world

| Aspects of the curriculum | Aspects of knowledge and understanding of the world | | | |
	Exploration and investigation	Designing and making skills	Information and communication technology	Sense of time, place, cultures and beliefs
Singing	Exploring the voice		Using microphones, tape-recorders, etc.	Singing songs from different times and places
Playing a range of instruments and sound-making materials	Exploring sound-making	Making and using instruments	Use of soundbeam, microphones, tape-recorders, etc.	Playing music from different times and places
Making up songs and music in response to a range of stimuli (including dance)	Exploring through improvised songs and music	Improvising and planning compositions	Use of ICT to create compositions and evaluate work	Using stimuli from different times and places
Listening to a range of live or recorded music	Identifying instruments from recordings	Making compilations of music, e.g. on a particular theme	Making compilations of music, e.g. on a particular theme Use of CD player, etc.	Listening to music from different times and places
Responding to music through the use of a range of creative media, including dance and spoken language Recording musical ideas in a range of forms or media	Representing ideas through movement, facial expression, other creative media and discussion Commenting on patterns	Making instruments or dances in response to music	Finding sounds on a computer or electronic keyboard that represent sounds heard	Using music from different times and places as stimuli

Conclusion

In this chapter we have explored the ways in which music is a tool for learning. The relationship between music and cognitive development has been explored. We have also outlined how music can support and is supported by each of the six areas of experience identified in the *Curriculum Guidance for the Foundation Stage* (QCA 2000). In Part 3, ways of supporting the curriculum are developed, firstly through establishing a music-rich environment and then through adult intervention.

Part 3

The role of adults

Creating a musical environment

In this chapter we outline the elements and characteristics of a supportive music environment. We have seen that music has much in common with language and we know that learning to talk is perhaps the most success-ful learning that any of us ever achieve. It therefore makes sense to look at how the environment in which children learn to talk supports their linguistic development, and then to see how that may be mirrored in creating an environment to support musical development.

A *language-rich environment*

We learn to talk in an environment that is informal, social, playful and loving. Babies themselves play with sounds, practising the elements that will make conversation possible. Ruth Weir, for example (1962), recorded her own baby's vocal play in the time she spent in her cot before falling asleep and discovered that she spent long periods playing with the pitch, rhythm and stress of words and phrases. Adults create a supportive environment by attributing meaning to babies' early utterances and actions, talking to babies as though they have spoken, long before they are able to do so (Wells and Nicholls 1985). They not only tolerate mistakes but recognize them as evidence of growing understanding. When a young child says 'goed' instead of 'went' we take this as a sign of developing awareness of the rules that govern past tense. In short, adults create an environment for learning to talk in which, according to Harrison and Pound (1996: 236):

- early efforts are strongly encouraged;
- every utterance is treated as if it had communicative intent;
- learning is informal;
- the rules of language use are learnt through talking and listening to others;
- babies and children hear adults all around them speaking the language fluently in a variety of ways and for a range of purposes;
- babies and children explore the possibilities of making vocal sounds;
- the emphasis is on communication rather than on acquiring technical skill for its own sake;
- babies and children themselves set the pace and the sequence of their own learning, though within a supportive structure provided by adults.

Concerns about low levels of literacy in many continents led researchers to seek ways of teaching children to read and write which would be more effective. Researchers in Australia and New Zealand were particularly successful in drawing on what is known about the development of spoken language and demonstrating ways in which a language-rich environment could be used to support not only the development of spoken language but also the development of literacy (Holdaway 1979; Temple *et al.* 1988). Their aim was that young children would be bathed in language. The culture of the classroom would be based on stories, narrative, books and poetry to such an extent that children could not help but be engaged by the excitement surrounding these activities. Holdaway (1980: 20) suggested a 'common sense environment' which would support literacy and include the following characteristics:

- a wide range of materials worthy of the children's attention and serving their life interests;
- materials bringing enrichment and joy to every child;
- children enjoying social support;
- children encouraged to operate independently;
- help and guidance readily available but without overbearing interference or correction;
- children taught self-correction and self-evaluation from the earliest stages;
- an environment free from threat.

Although Holdaway was writing over 20 years ago, the effectiveness of this general approach continues to be confirmed by teachers, psychologists and neuroscientists. Tyrrell (2001), a reception class teacher, describes a classroom where children's imagination supports the process of learning to read, through the provision of an atmosphere where story creates an exciting and stimulating learning environment. The prime importance of playfulness is also supported in the work of developmental psychologists such as Harris (2000). He argues that imagination and emotion are indispensable to learning. The work of neurophysiologists such as Siegel (1999) also underlines the fundamental importance of emotion, playfulness and interaction with others in the learning process.

A *music-rich environment*

The similarities between language and music outlined in Chapter 3 would suggest that there are common features in the two learning processes. It is no coincidence that similar characteristics to those outlined above have been identified by researchers and by musicians themselves as contributing to successful musical development. Sloboda (1994) identifies preconditions for high musical achievement which can be summarized as follows:

- musical stimulation in infancy;
- long periods of engagement in the chosen musical activity;
- family support;
- early teaching that stresses the fun of music;
- opportunities for emotional responses to music.

In a survey of the learning processes of successful musicians, Harrison and Pound (1996: 235) identified a number of common characteristics demonstrated in the home environment in which musicians grew up. Table 5.1 sets out these home characteristics. The right-hand column suggests ways in which parents, carers and practitioners in group settings can draw on these characteristics to create a music-rich environment.

North American teacher and researcher Rena Upitis (1990, 1992) has written extensively about environments which allow children to become engrossed in musical activity. She describes a music-rich environment which she terms a 'music playground'. She identifies eight features of a supportive environment which, although aimed at older children, are highly relevant to work with young children. The following list is based on her suggestions (Upitis 1992: 248):

- an emphasis on the processes of learning;
- a nurturing atmosphere in which it is safe to take risks;
- choice and collaboration are encouraged;
- physically inviting;
- integrated activities;

Table 5.1 The home environment of musicians and ways in which a music-rich environment can be created

Common characteristics of successful musicians	Creating a music-rich environment at home or in a group setting
The musicians usually grew up in a musical environment	All children are born musical, so even if their earliest months or years have not been spent in an explicitly musical environment, it is never too late to stimulate their musicality
From an early age they heard and saw music as part of everyday life	Adults need to create an environment where music is seen as a normal part of everyday experience, integrated into the life of the home, school or nursery so that it is not seen as difficult or threatening
Many of the adults with whom they came into contact were musically active	This may be difficult for adults who do not regard themselves as musical and who lack confidence in their own music-making. Nevertheless it is important that all adults are seen by children to engage in musical activity and not to leave it to specialists. It is more important to be seen to be doing it than to be good at it
It was expected that all children would develop as musicians	In many areas it is clear that expectations play an important part in raising achievement and this is equally true in music. In our culture, there has been a tendency to expect only the 'gifted few' to be successful in music, whereas research shows that all are born musical and can achieve success if given appropriate opportunities and encouragement
They often had informal access to instruments	Even if children do not have access to conventional instruments, they will explore the sounds made by pots and spoons, paper bags, cardboard tubes, etc. A music-rich environment must place a strong emphasis on offering children a wide range of sound-makers (including conventional instruments where possible) to explore, and the time and space in which to do so. Adults' encouragement of these explorations is an important part of the developmental process

Table 5.1 Continued

Common characteristics of successful musicians	Creating a music-rich environment at home or in a group setting
They had time to explore both the expressive and technical aspects of music-making	As we have seen, children very quickly acquire some understanding of the relationship between music and the expression of emotion. Adults need to reinforce this connection in their choice of materials and in their support for children's independent music-making
They were allowed to join in the general music-making	Young children need little encouragement to join in group music-making, particularly where adults are seen to be enjoying it. They should be offered plenty of opportunities to do so, both in group situations and in more informal ways when engaged in other activities. Whether or not children are singing or playing an instrument, they need to be allowed to be physically active as their ability to listen and engage with music is improved through physical activity
They had early opportunities for playing and singing alongside others with a variety of expertise	Community involvement of adults and other children will help to provide opportunities for children to see and hear a range of expertise. Children's enjoyment of musical performances is enhanced where there is an element of participation. Young children's need for physical engagement in music should be recognized
The initial emphasis in their music-making was on enjoyment rather than on acquiring technical skill	All learning is enhanced by enjoyment. The chemistry in the brain when children are having fun promotes learning. A music-rich environment must place an emphasis on enjoyment and pleasure. It should be sufficiently safe and supportive for children to feel able to take risks and make mistakes

- adults act as resources;
- children can create their own structures for learning;
- multiple ways of interacting with the materials, e.g. visual, aural, kinaesthetic.

Creating a musical atmosphere

We have already discussed how music is an important means of communication with very young children. Adults living and working with children under 3 years of age find that singing and other forms of musical play are helpful strategies in communicating with such young children. Papousek (1994) suggests that parents and carers stop singing with infants and toddlers at too early a stage. The reason for this is unclear but, as we have discussed in Chapter 3, the widespread availability of recorded music may inhibit adults' singing. Some parents may feel that it is more beneficial for their children to listen to recorded music than to be subjected to their poor singing. Whatever the cause, the effect is to curtail an important learning strategy. Where adults do continue to sing both improvised and known songs with young children, they make an important contribution to the creation of a positive musical environment. Goldschmied and Jackson (1994: 108) affirm this:

> It is far better to show children that singing can be spontaneous and informal. Children love made-up songs about themselves and the things they do every day. This is something the key person can do regularly in her small group.

Shila, Wayne's key person, picked him up from his cot as he woke, crying. She gently cradled him, soothing his crying and murmuring in his ear, 'We'll soon have you clean and dry.' She repeated this phrase several times as she moved towards the changing table, varying the rhythm and intonation. In another group of 1–2-year-olds, as children were sitting on the carpet playing with farmyard animals, Kemi began to sing 'ee-i-ee-i-o' repeatedly. The practitioner joined in singing 'Kemi and Jamie had a farm'. Children took it in turns to initiate additional verses.

As children grow older, this informal musical play remains important. Often when children are engaged in activities such as playing with dough they will enjoy singing with other children around the table. Sometimes these are made-up songs and sometimes they are known favourites. In this spontaneous play, children may sometimes use everyday objects to make sounds to accompany their singing or movement. They may also want to take musical instruments to use in other parts of the environment and it can be a good idea to have some readily available for this purpose.

However, staff will need to agree a consistent policy so that children are clear about what is permissible and what is not. For instance, some instruments will be damaged if they are used in the water tray but might be used to good effect in the dressing up area.

With all age groups, use of song and music at group times or at particular routines contributes to a musical environment. Welcome songs are commonly used with very young children or in special education and provide a focus for coming together and a signal that the day is about to start. In some settings a song may signal storytime or clearing up time. Even if this is not the case, many children themselves initiate their own chanting to mark the occasion as they call out 'storytime, storytime' to one another.

Music is frequently used to create a sense of group cohesion. As children gather on the carpet for a story, songs may be used to encourage others to hurry to join the class. Where children are off task, songs can be very effective in encouraging them to share a focus with the rest of the class. Young children may be helped to behave appropriately in a situation which some may find difficult. A group of young nursery children were waiting to attend a whole-school event. In order to keep them calm and interested, the teacher improvised a song with movements that mentioned children by name, reminding them of what was going to happen and encouraging them to join in.

Some practitioners use a chord on the piano, a single strike on a triangle or a drum rhythm to signal a change in routine or a particular event. Children quickly become used to such signals and often respond well to them. Such procedures are demonstrating to children some of the functions of music in the wider world. Music is commonly used in this way, but it is important that it is not only used in this way. As Hildebrandt (1998: 69) reminds us:

> Unlike other areas of the curriculum, where exploration and experimentation are encouraged, the main focus of music time is often to get everybody to do the same thing at the same time and do it well. Even though many teachers would like to believe that they are using music as a vehicle for creative expression, what they are actually doing is using music to control children's behavior.

Recorded music

Recorded music cannot replace live interaction. The constant playing of music, whether on CDs, radio or television, with no quiet periods, might even discourage children's own music-making. However, if it is used thoughtfully, recorded music can make a helpful contribution to the creation of a musical environment. It can create an atmosphere for particular types of activity or at certain times of day. At the end of a long day, children attending extended daycare provision might enjoy some soothing music as they relax before going home.

At periods when children are actively engaged in a range of activities, some background music may support concentration. Tapes of familiar songs can be used to encourage children to join in. Smidt (1998: 95) suggests 'putting a tape-recorder with a selection of taped music in the home corner'. Children might enjoy bringing tapes from home to share with other children as they play. Recordings of rhythmic or atmospheric music might stimulate children to dance or to develop instrumental accompaniments. However, adults must make a judgement about whether this music has become intrusive or is limiting other kinds of interaction. If children cannot make themselves heard above the music, its presence is unhelpful.

At a nursery school, staff developed a small room which they called a sensory room. Unlike the high-tech sensory rooms often found in special schools, this is furnished with cushions and fabrics. Interesting small objects with a variety of textures are placed around the room to appeal to the sense of touch. The windows are shaded, low voltage lamps are used and spotlights focus on mirror balls. Scented oils and aromatic plants stimulate the sense of smell, while a tape-recorder plays whale songs and other atmospheric music. Wind chimes are hung at different heights, so that children can manipulate the lower ones. Small changes are frequently made to the environment, maintaining a balance between the novel and the familiar. The integration of music with other sensory experiences makes a strong contribution to the overall atmosphere. In the *Curriculum Guidance for the Foundation Stage* (QCA 2000: 117), practitioners are reminded that 'creative development requires children to learn to express with all of their senses', and this is a good example of how this can be facilitated.

Time and space for music-making

Children cannot learn all they need to know about music through organized sessions. Free access to music resources over extended periods is therefore an indispensable part of creating an environment that will support music-making. In the relevant section of the *Curriculum Guidance for the Foundation Stage* (QCA 2000) relating to creative development, there is a strong emphasis on the importance of ensuring that children have sufficient time and space in which to be creative. The document emphasizes that children's creativity develops over time and takes time, and that therefore children must be given time to work at their own pace and to explore and develop new ideas. It also acknowledges that space is required for the development of creative ideas. This is consistent with Sloboda's (1994) finding that successful musicians spent long periods of time engaged in their chosen musical activity.

Adults' attitudes

Adults play a critical role in creating a musical atmosphere. It is they who place an emphasis on fun and playfulness (Sloboda 1994; Harrison and Pound 1996), who create the nurturing atmosphere in which children can feel able to take the risks which lead to creativity (Upitis 1992; QCA 2000), and where choice and collaboration are fostered (Upitis 1992).

All of this is reinforced by the *Curriculum Guidance for the Foundation Stage* (QCA 2000), where guidance is given for supporting creative development. Practitioners are reminded of the importance of allowing children to develop their own ideas:

> [Creativity] begins with curiosity and involves children in exploration and experimentation . . . They make decisions, take risks and play with ideas. Children's creativity . . . is best facilitated by adults who sensitively support this process and do not dominate it . . .
>
> Creativity is not about pleasing adults or producing adult-determined art, music or dance . . .
>
> The practitioner must create a climate where curiosity is encouraged and where children can experience the unexpected.
>
> (QCA 2000: 118)

Nothing is of more importance in establishing a music-rich environment than adults, both at home and in group settings, who believe in children's abilities, who support and encourage children in their journey of musical discovery.

An environment to support music learning

Indoors

Most nursery settings have a music area alongside other areas of provision such as a book area, a block area, dressing up and so on. It is an area where resources are gathered for music-making and where both adults and children can go to select an instrument, a piece of recorded music or a songbook. Although music areas have a great deal of potential for fun and exploration, all too often they become neglected. It is possible to avoid this by ensuring that:

- resources are well maintained and attractively arranged;
- regular changes are made to the content and presentation of the materials;

- adults spend time (both planned and spontaneous) working with children in this area;
- the area is organized in such a way that children know how to keep it tidy, to replace resources so that others can find them;
- there is always a balance of familiar and unfamiliar materials;
- visual resources are used to supplement the music-making;
- the area is big enough for small groups of children to move rhythmically or expressively;
- the area is located where it will be used but will not disturb others – this may mean that it cannot be used all the time, but there should be extensive periods when children will have free access to it.

A well-equipped music area might contain:

- instruments and sound-making materials;
- tapes, tape-recorder and headphones;
- songbooks, words and scores;
- writing materials;
- a range of visual materials.

The choices made will depend on the age of the children, the amount of space available and other curriculum foci. For example, decisions about what to provide for a group of toddlers will be different from provision made for a group of 6-year-olds. Similarly, if the music area is very small, only a limited range of music-making equipment can be offered, but it should be changed frequently. If the curriculum focus is transport, then resources may be selected to encourage music-making around that theme.

Over time, practitioners should aim to include the following range of materials and resources in their planned provision.

1 Instruments and sound making materials
Children should have access to:

- instruments made from a variety of materials (e.g. wood, metal, skin);
- instruments played in different ways (e.g. beaten, scraped, shaken, blown);
- untuned and tuned instruments;
- instruments from a variety of cultures;
- instruments they have made themselves;
- everyday objects that make interesting sounds, some of which may be provided by adults and some discovered by children.

Everyday objects are particularly interesting because they encourage children to explore the sound potential of things around them. Hildebrandt (1998: 72) relates the following story:

One day, a five-year-old said, 'Hey! do you wanna hear me play my coat?' He plucked a button on his coat and, sure enough, it made a great sound. After teaching Sharon (his teacher) how to play it, he suddenly stopped. A look of wonder came across his face. '*Now* I get it!' he exclaimed. '*Anything* can be a musical instrument!'

Treasure basket collections provided for heuristic play for babies and toddlers include many items which support the exploration of sound and this should be encouraged in the same way as other forms of sensory exploration.

2 Tapes, tape-recorder and headphones

Children will enjoy making recordings of their own music-making. A tape-recorder with a built-in microphone will enable this to happen and they will often need little encouragement to start using it to record their own songs and instrumental explorations. This has the added advantage of enabling parents to hear what their child has been doing.

Children should also have opportunities to listen to songs and music from a wide range of sources and styles. This can include recordings of their own singing and music-making as well as those made professionally. Children can be helped to accept and enjoy an increasingly wide range of music if we help them to make connections between what we offer them and what they already know. They can be assisted in doing so by having new music introduced in the following ways:

- music using familiar instruments played in a different style;
- music using instruments related to those with which children are familiar, e.g. gamelan, marimba, tabla, talking drums, Latin percussion;
- music that relates to their own explorations, e.g. fast music, quiet music, creepy music;
- music on a familiar topic or theme;
- music for a familiar purpose, e.g. festival, birthday, nursery rhyme.

Adults should be aware that the tapes provided with songbooks are not always appropriate for use with children. They are generally intended to familiarize staff with the tunes and may be pitched too high for children's voices.

3 Songbooks, words and scores

The repertoire of songs should include:

- action songs, game songs and rhymes;
- ring games;
- songs that tell stories;
- songs involving repetition;

- songs from a variety of styles and cultures, and in different languages;
- nursery rhymes.

Adults might like to make some songbooks available for children, as they enjoy browsing through them. However, if favourite songs are written out on a card or in small home-made books with illustrations that help children to remember what the song is, then these cards and books may be a good stimulus for singing and can also be used for listening in conjunction with tapes.

Since most songbooks will use standard western notation they will not provide children with the opportunity to become familiar with other notational forms. From time to time it may be helpful, therefore, to display some alternative forms of notation (see Harrison 2001).

4 *Writing materials*
Some children may enjoy using pencils, felt-tip pens, and paper to:

- draw pictures or symbols stimulated by music they are listening to;
- draw the instruments;
- record their musical ideas;
- imitate notations;
- make songbooks.

5 A *range of stimulus materials*
In the music area, a range of visual materials, which could include the following, may be displayed:

- pictures of instruments, musicians and dancers;
- musical scores of various kinds;
- pictures, paintings, photographs and artefacts to stimulate children's own music-making, such as pictures of waterfalls or a bustling market scene.

Stories and poems can often stimulate music-making, sometimes because adults have modelled this in group story sessions. Even before children can read, well-loved books or poetry cards may encourage children to make up songs or music based on this familiar material.

A playgroup leader describes her music area in the following way, underlining the fact that provision need not be expensive:

We now have a music corner and have in there our tape recorder and a selection of tapes. We have a range of musical instruments (bought out of the proceeds of our last jumble sale). We have a 'music collage'. This is a large piece of card on which we have stuck things that will make a sound. We have a piece of corrugated card with a lollipop stick hanging next to it on a piece of string; milk bottle tops which jangle against each other; and a range of other things to bang, pluck, scrape and rattle.

(cited in Smidt 1998: 98–9)

Outdoors

Outdoor provision has long been recognized as an important part of early childhood education. The advantages of working and playing outdoors include children's general health and well-being as well as the opportunities to work on a larger scale than is possible indoors, make more noise and observe or explore the effects of natural phenomena like the wind. In engaging in similar activities both indoors and out, children are helped to see connections between different experiences and learning activities. Therefore in addition to offering the same musical activities that have been provided indoors, it is important to offer musical experiences that take advantage of the possibility of using large equipment and making loud noises and encourage children to explore sounds made by wind, rain, trees and water.

Powell (2001: 63) suggests that gardens may be planted in such a way as to provide a range of sound-makers. She suggests:

- plants with large leaves (such as *Fatsia japonica, Musa basjoo* or *Rheum palmatum*) 'so you can enjoy the sound of the rain playing tom-tom on their leaves';
- plants which rustle (such as bamboo or grasses) or (like *Rhinanthus minor*) rattle in the wind;
- plants with exploding seed pods, such as *Genista tinctoria, Ulex europaeus* and *Cytisus scoparius*;
- 'different materials underfoot';
- 'twiggy shrubs and bushes such as cornus, hazel and willow close to fences, so they'll clatter against them';
- attracting wildlife that generates sound into the garden by planting trees and shrubs that are inviting to birds and insects. She suggests that you 'visit Flora for Fauna's website for inspiration (www.nhm. ac.uk/science/projects/fff/intro.htm)'.

Bilton (1998) suggests creating a simple outside music area. However, it is possible to go beyond this and offer a wider range of resources that are too bulky or noisy to be easily used indoors. Steel pans or timpani, gongs or large cymbals can be very exciting for young children. Providing them in the outdoor area allows children to explore the full range of sound-making possibilities. However, these are very expensive and easily damaged. Equally stimulating experiences can be provided using household objects or found materials not specifically designed for music-making (Ouvry, in press). These can take the form of installations or collections.

Installations

Tony Dale (1995: 20) describes his idea in constructing an outdoor installation for a special school. He wanted to make, he says, 'outdoor instruments to spark into life the potential for music-making . . . without the need for any supervision or for structured music sessions'.

Musical installations can take a variety of forms. The simplest form may be wind chimes. A wide variety is available commercially, but children can also make effective wind chimes themselves with adult help. Wind chimes can be made from a variety of materials – bamboo, metal, plastic, glass, stone, shell, foil, clay – all of which make different and interesting sounds. They can be hung high in a tree where they can be operated only by the wind, or they can be placed at a lower level or given a long cord so that they can be operated by children.

Relatively simple installations can be created by attaching sound-making materials to a fixed or portable framework. This may be as simple as a wooden clothes horse, a fence or a tree, or could be a designer-made structure such as a pyramid or cube. On the framework can be hung or attached a range of materials. These could include flower pots of different sizes, saucepans and their lids, frying pans, different lengths of plastic or copper piping. A row of adjacent bamboo canes can be used as a scraper. Hollow tubes stuck in the ground can be covered with plastic heads and played like drums. If the installation is large enough, water butts and buckets may be attached to it as they make an impressive sound. Some climbing frames and playgrounds also have fixed musical equipment such as a large-sized metallophone or xylophone, or sound mats which make different sounds as different parts of the mat are walked or jumped on. Some schools have employed designers to create more complex structures.

Children express enthusiasm for these outdoor instruments. The children of Smallberry Green Primary School, Isleworth (1997: 25) are quoted as saying:

> I like the snake best. My favourite way of making the sound is banging it.
>
> (Bahador, aged 4)

> I like the face down silver tubes. I like the sound it makes it is nice. I also like the golden tree pattern on the top. I like the sizzling snake. Everything is set out nicely.
>
> (Jimmy, aged 5)

I like the snake and the xylophone. I like the beaters. I like the slap drums as well.

(Jessica, aged 5)

Teachers are also enthusiastic about outdoor structures:

The children love them. They find their own way to play the chimes and gain much pleasure from them. What we find most exciting is that the instrument has become a focus of shared activity.

(Dale 1995: 20)

Collections
Installations, whether permanent or temporary, have been designed by adults who have determined the possibilities for music-making. Collections of household objects and found materials or outdoor musical instruments allow children to make choices and decisions and more freely initiate their own explorations of the sound-making potential. Some of the items mentioned above, like water butts, buckets and saucepans, would also be appropriate here. The collection might include long lengths of plastic drainpiping or carpet tubes, which can be played by bouncing them on the ground, hitting them with a flat object such as a table tennis bat, or blowing down them. It is also possible to buy sets of tuned plastic tubes. Other items might include plastic bottles or other containers filled with different types of materials or different amounts of water.

Movement area

Because of the close link between music and movement in young children's development, an area large enough to allow large-scale movement can be provided to support musical development. Movement areas may be located both indoors and out and should be closely linked to music provision. Post and Hohmann (2000: 177) recommend that a movement area for toddlers should include a wide range of equipment to support gross motor development alongside:

- rattles, shakers
- bells
- xylophone and mallet
- metallophone and mallet
- sturdy bongo drum or floor drum
- tambourine
- small, sturdy rainstick

- music recordings
- CD or cassette player.

Children benefit from being able to observe their own movements. A large expanse of safety mirror in the movement area allows children to 'watch themselves and get visual feedback to their responses to music' (Achilles 1999: 21). A study by Andress (1991) reinforces the importance of children being able to gain feedback through the use of mirrors. She suggests that where adults model a wide range of types of movement, describe what children are doing and make suggestions for further movements, children's musical understanding is enhanced. She stresses the importance of this happening informally in order to allow children to respond in ways which match their level of experience and maturity.

A soundbeam is well-suited for use in a movement area such as that described above. As indicated earlier, this equipment is particularly valuable for children with physical disabilities which limit their movement. It needs to be placed in an area which is not used as a thoroughfare. In the same way as mirrors provide visual feedback, a soundbeam provides aural feedback, as even tiny movements will register a change in sound.

A nursery school has created an outdoor stage area for spontaneous performance of music or dance and organized musical activities such as ring games. Children use it as an integral part of their outdoor play, dancing, playing musical instruments and role-playing pop stars. Sometimes there is music playing on a portable cassette player and a selection of hand-held instruments may be available. At other times, children may dance on their own or bring with them home-made instruments from the classroom. Activity from the classroom may also spill over into outdoor play when children use dressing-up clothes or other props to support their play.

Flexible use of the environment

Upitis (1992) stresses the importance of a workshop approach which allows children to use a range of tools and resources in different situations. A child may move from the music area where he or she has been listening to a tape and playing an instrument, to the creative workshop. There, he or she can make an instrument from junk material, decorate it with fabrics and coloured papers, and then move outdoors to play the instrument as part of a group game. This sequence of activities supports concentration, helps the child to make connections between different areas of learning and promotes independent learning.

In addition, the resources in the music areas, both indoors and out, are mirrored and may be explored in other areas of the classroom. Saucepans in the home corner, an enamel jug in the water tray, the rustle of different kinds of paper or fabric, leaves underfoot in the garden, all provide aural stimulation. Children should be encouraged to listen to, compare and explore the sounds produced.

Community

Parents, carers and the local community are an invaluable musical resource. Young children's families often have their own musical traditions and expertise and it is important that their skills and enthusiasms are brought into the group setting. Since culture plays such an important part in the development of musical competence, it is essential not to create any gap between music-making at home and music-making in the school or nursery. Parents can teach songs or come in to perform on an instrument. Older brothers and sisters may enjoy coming to perform for a small group of children. Children need to see and hear musicians with a range of expertise in order to understand that music-making is an activity that can be undertaken successfully and provide enjoyment whatever the competence of the performer. Staff who may not think of themselves as musical should be encouraged to join in the general music-making. In doing so, they act as a role model for children, demonstrating that music is something that everyone can do and enjoy. As with singing to babies, it is more important to do it than to be good at it. Moreover, as music is a developmental activity, by taking part, the adults will get better at it.

Professional musicians can also make a valuable contribution to creating a musical environment. They can inspire children through their expertise as musicians and performers. However, schools or nurseries should ensure that musicians they engage are aware of the needs of young children and are able to present their performances accordingly. Similar considerations will apply when deciding which public performances are appropriate for children to attend.

A professional drummer who lives near one school volunteers to come every morning to the nursery to accompany both group and informal singing. Children also select instruments and join in with him, watching and imitating his movements.

Suthers (1993) describes a project in which young children from the age of 5 are invited to attend performances of a symphony orchestra. She describes the benefits of the programme as follows:

Live performance adds a dimension to a program of musical listening

Musicians from the community promoting children's enthusiasm for music

Table 5.2 Relationships between aspects of the music curriculum and aspects of the environment

Aspects of the curriculum	Aspects of the environment/resources
Singing	• Repertoire of songs; recordings and songbooks; including songs from different cultures; involve the community in identifying appropriate songs • Role modelling by adults
Playing a range of instruments and sound-making materials	• Instruments – blowing, plucking, scraping, striking, shaking; different materials – wood, metal, plastic, natural materials • Household or everyday objects – saucepans, buckets, flowerpots, spoons, plastic bottles and containers, different materials • Scrap materials, glue, scissors, staplers, sellotape, etc. • Large-scale scrap material for outdoor exploration, e.g. drainpiping, water butts • Space to do this, e.g. music corner, outdoor area; space to make, space to perform • Wind chimes, different sizes and materials • Role modelling by adults
Making up songs and music in response to a range of stimuli (including dance)	• Capturing children's made-up songs and music – tape-recorder and microphones • Stimulus materials – pictures, artefacts, a range of appropriate stories and poems, video/film • Examples of songs and music to act as models – cultural variety, range of expertise (including other children, songs/music made up by adults) • Soundbeam
Listening to a range of live or recorded music	• Live music performances • Range of recorded music • Videos of musical performances • Tape-recorders, headsets, CD/sound system, video camera, video player
Responding to music through the use of a range of creative media, including dance and spoken language Recording musical ideas in a range of forms or media	• Live music performances • Range of recorded music • Space for movement • Opportunities for small group conversation • Good access to art materials • Materials to support dance, e.g. fabrics, ankle bells • Soundbeam • Examples of notated music – wide variety, including graphic scores • Tape-recorder, video-recorder

that is not possible through recordings. To *see* the musicians play their instruments, to *hear* the sounds they make, to *watch* the conductor perform and *become aware of the interactions* between different players and *observe the patterns* in the music, is to really experience the orchestra.

(Suthers 1993: 55)

The environment and the curriculum

An effective environment for music must be able to support all aspects of the music curriculum as identified in Chapter 3. Table 5.2 indicates how elements of the environment relate to each aspect.

Conclusion

A music-rich environment will include indoor and outdoor provision. It will enable children to use musical equipment in a variety of contexts and will promote curiosity and enjoyment of making and responding to sounds and music. Adults play an important part in this process. They act as role models and determine the ethos of the setting. They have responsibility for keeping the environment attractive and stimulating. In the next chapter we look more closely at the role of the adult in actively planning and leading musical activities.

6

Intervention and support

No teaching strategies, formal or informal, can succeed unless they are based on an understanding of how children generate their own musical ideas.

(Glover 2000: 40)

In the previous chapter, the importance of creating a music-rich environment was stressed. However, no matter how stimulating the environment, musical learning, like learning to talk, relies heavily on the involvement of others, because it is in essence a form of communication. In this chapter, the role of adults in all aspects of musical activity is outlined. As in previous chapters, the importance of all adults being involved is emphasized since any indication to children that music is for the gifted few will lower their expectations of themselves.

Developing confidence in ourselves as musicians

In order to create a music-rich environment, it is essential that all adults are involved so that music can be fully integrated into the life of the home, school or nursery. Children need to see that everyone, whatever their level of expertise, can take part in, and enjoy, making music. Being prepared to sing with children, or to have a go on instruments, or to dance in response to music, will all offer enormous encouragement to children. In contrast, if some adults are seen to be reluctant to do these things, or to express lack of confidence in their ability to do so, children will be discouraged.

However, it is unfortunately the case that many adults do lack confidence in their own musical ability. Since we are all born musical, this is unlikely to be due to a lack of musicality. It is much more likely to be the result of our education, and it is very important that we do not replicate this situation with the young children with whom we live and work.

Even adults who think of themselves as unmusical have a lot more musical experience than very young children. Most of us have listened to large quantities of music, and have a knowledge and understanding of several musical styles or genres. We can tell the difference between opera and rap! We can probably remember in our heads hundreds of tunes of familiar songs. We can usually remember the tunes better than we can the words.

Some people are not confident about being able to sing these tunes, and may even describe themselves as tone deaf. This term is very inaccurate, as it implies that, because of a hearing deficiency, a person is inherently unmusical. For the vast majority of people who have difficulty singing, this is not the case, and even these supposedly tone deaf people have no trouble hearing differences in pitch when listening to, say, recorded music. All of us, with few exceptions, can learn to sing in tune, and where people have difficulty in doing so it is far more likely to be the result of lack of practice at controlling the movement of the voice. Sometimes this has resulted from an early experience, such as being told not to sing by a teacher at school or by a member of one's family. Such experiences can have a devastating effect on the singer's confidence, with the result that they may stop trying to sing and therefore never learn how to control their voices. Other people may sing perfectly well, but not like the sound of their voice (perhaps somebody has told them they made an awful row). Others have low voices and their inability to hit the high notes has led them to doubt their musicality.

In general, these are not considerations that need to bother us when we are working with young children. Children are far more likely to be enthused by our singing than distressed by the quality of our voices. Nor are we likely to give children 'bad habits' by singing in the wrong key or making a mistake with the tune. If we are singing familiar songs, children will learn them from a number of different sources. There are even instances of children 'correcting' versions of a song they have learnt from a teacher who deviated from the accepted tune.

Another common expression of lack of confidence is 'I've got no sense of rhythm' or 'I can't keep in time'. Again, very few people have a physical difficulty that prevents them doing so. Virtually all of us can tap our feet along with music we listen to. Most lack of rhythmic accuracy stems from anxiety or inhibition when we are asked to do something in a formal situation.

Other instances of lack of musical confidence are expressed in phrases like 'I'm not a musician because I can't read music', or 'I can't play by ear', or 'I'm no good at music – I can't play an instrument'. All of these statements could equally be made by some well respected musicians. For instance, Paul McCartney famously does not read music, many classically trained musicians cannot play without music and find the idea of doing so quite daunting. Many professional singers are unable to play instruments and many professional instrumentalists are not accomplished singers.

However, although there are few natural barriers to making music, the confidence barrier still has to be addressed. If parents or others working with children lack confidence, the strategies below may help:

- Use the tapes that come with songbooks, singing along with them until you are confident that you know the tune.
- Get a friend or colleague to teach you a song, so that you can sing it confidently.
- Work alongside a more confident colleague, acting as a joint leader in group activities, until you have the confidence to lead on your own.
- If your school or nursery employs a music specialist, take some time to join in the activities, observing and working alongside the specialist so that you develop your own skills.
- Be prepared to explore music-making with voice and instruments alongside children, joining in their journey of discovery and increasing your own understanding in the process.
- Try out a new activity with a small group of children first before using it with a large group or whole class.

Observing children

Most early years' practitioners are skilled at observing and use observation as a day-to-day tool for assessing and planning. The strategies and procedures that are used to observe other areas of the curriculum will serve equally well for music. Some practitioners (and even parents who know their children well) feel that they do not have the skills to recognize significant developments in young children's music-making or to identify musically able children. However, as Achilles (1999: 23) reminds us: 'Because observation of children is a hallmark of early childhood education practice, describing children's responses to music is a skill that caregivers already possess.'

Chapter 2 in this book gives an indication of what is significant in young children's musical development. As the chapter makes clear, musical development is so bound up with experience that there are no clear answers to the question of what 'normal' development looks like. Observations and discussions with colleagues will help to clarify views and to arrive at a set of expectations shared by the team. Practitioners will also have a broad understanding of creative development in general which will help to shape a shared view. Table 6.1 gives a general picture of what to look for in different aspects of the music curriculum.

Children may not demonstrate all the behaviours listed in the table. Their responses will vary according to age, their personality and their home background. For instance, if a child is keen to share with an adult a song they have made up, this may be an indication of social confidence rather than musical ability. Similarly, a child who explores an instrument imaginatively or creates recognizable rhythm patterns may simply have had more opportunities to play instruments at home and therefore be more confident. Both confidence and sociability are, however, important in music-making. As Gardner (1993a) suggests, being musical entails more than just musical intelligence – it also requires interpersonal competence and self-awareness (or, as he calls it, intrapersonal intelligence).

Identifying musically gifted children

There is a strong political interest in identifying children who are gifted and talented. Music is one of the areas singled out for identification and support amongst older children. While musical prodigies do exist, it is important to remember, firstly, that children develop in different ways, and secondly that even prodigies have to 'put in the hours' (Sloboda, cited in Mihill 1993). Children with high musical ability may demonstrate many of the characteristics outlined in Table 6.1 earlier than other children. They may also demonstrate some of the characteristics outlined in the QCA guidance (QCA 2001a) which was referred to in Chapter 2. However, expressions of interest or confidence in music-making may be as much the result of greater encouragement and experience at home as of a superior innate ability for music. We should do nothing to discourage any child from making music, but we should be cautious about making assumptions about musical ability until all children have had opportunities to engage in musical activity and demonstrate their enthusiasm, interest and competence. Only a minority of expert musicians have been prodigies (Sloboda and Davidson 1996), and not all prodigies turn out to be expert musicians.

Planning

Guidance has been published by the QCA entitled *Planning for Learning in the Foundation Stage* (QCA 2001b). It provides a range of models for

Table 6.1 Indicators of musical development with respect to the different aspects of the music curriculum

Aspect of the curriculum	What to look for
Singing	<ul><li>Are they interested when they hear singing?</li><li>Do they attempt to join in with actions?</li><li>Do they join in instantly recognizable or catchy parts of the song?</li><li>Do they initiate singing themselves?</li><li>Do they explore different ways of using their voices?</li><li>Does their singing begin to have rhythmic and melodic shape?</li><li>Can they sing familiar songs from memory?</li><li>Do they enjoy singing alone and with others?</li><li>Do they learn new songs readily?</li></ul>
Playing a range of instruments and sound-making materials	<ul><li>Are they interested when they hear sounds and instruments?</li><li>Do they explore sources of sound?</li><li>Are they interested in joining in when they see or hear music being played?</li><li>Do their explorations begin to show shape or pattern?</li><li>Do they explore different ways of playing instruments and sound-makers?</li><li>Do they enjoy making music alone and with others?</li></ul>
Making up songs and music in response to a range of stimuli (including dance)	<ul><li>Do they improvise songs or musical phrases while engaged in other activities?</li><li>Do they play around with familiar songs, e.g. changing the words, embellishing the tune, varying the rhythm?</li><li>Do they play around with sounds they have heard, e.g. phrases spoken by someone else, sounds in the environment etc.?</li><li>Do they approach adults with songs of their own?</li><li>Do they explore different ways of using voices and instruments?</li><li>Do they explore sound-makers imaginatively and over sustained periods of time?</li><li>Are they interested in sharing their explorations with an adult?</li></ul>

Table 6.1 Continued

Aspect of the curriculum	What to look for
	• Do they contribute ideas to group music-making activities such as creating musical illustrations to stories? • Can they make associations between sounds and pictures? • Can they link sounds to physical movement?
Responding to music through the use of a range of creative media, including dance and spoken language Recording musical ideas in a range of forms or media	• Are they interested in listening to music? • Do they make physical or vocal responses to music? • Do they express their ideas about music either through physical movement or spoken language? • Are they able to move rhythmically in response to music? • Are they able to express ideas about music in other symbolic media?
Listening to a range of live or recorded music	• Do they show interest and enjoyment when they hear music? • Do they recognize tunes or music that they have heard before? • Do they demonstrate that they remember songs or music by singing them later? • Are they interested in listening to music they have not heard before? • Do they ask to listen to particular pieces of music?

planning which cover all six areas of learning in the Foundation Stage. Unfortunately, given the importance of music and the way in which it supports other areas of learning, none of the examples includes any reference to musical activities. When using the guidance it is important to ensure that music takes its place alongside other elements of provision.

The guidance rightly places an emphasis on the importance of observation in planning. In observing children's musical activity and addressing the questions in Table 6.1, practitioners will be identifying aspects of the curriculum that need to be planned for. In general, the younger the children that you are working with, the more likely it is that you will be planning for them as individuals. As children grow older, planning is more likely to focus on the group as a whole, with some differentiation for specific groups or individual children. Whatever the age group, opportunities to make music both alone and with peers and adults need to be provided.

Planning for intervention and development of learning will also focus on:

- child-initiated activities;
- adult-responsive activities;
- adult-directed activities.

Again, the balance between the different kinds of activity or experience will vary according to the age group and their experience.

Child-initiated activities

As stated in the previous chapter, adults play an important role in creating an environment in which children feel able to initiate activity. Adult intervention in relation to child-initiated activities consists of creating an environment and climate for learning that enables children to feel secure, to explore freely, to take risks and to interact with others. As suggested in Chapter 3, the younger the child, the more heavily learning depends on child-initiated activities and experiences. In Chapter 5, the characteristics of a music-rich environment were outlined. Planning for child-initiated activity should focus on ensuring that, over time, children are given the opportunity to engage with the full range of musical activity and exploration. This will include planning to ensure that the environment remains stimulating. This means that staff should plan to keep the music area inviting, introduce new material and watch to see that children are not losing interest in existing provision.

Table 6.2 identifies some of the activities which children may initiate in relation to each aspect of the music curriculum.

It is vital that adults also join in spontaneously with what children are doing and, through their enthusiasm and interest, reinforce learning. Adults should observe what is happening and use their observations to plan both adult-responsive and adult-directed activities.

Adult-responsive activities

It is sometimes difficult to tell whether an activity is child-initiated or adult-responsive, because adults who work with young children are sensitive to children's intentions. Nevertheless, the distinction is important because it is through engaging with adults' responses that children are

Table 6.2 Child-initiated activities in relation to each aspect of the music curriculum

Aspects of the curriculum	Child-initiated activities: free play and exploration
Singing	Spontaneous singing of both familiar and invented songs in any area of the classroom or nursery, indoors or out
Playing a range of instruments and sound-making materials	Spontaneous playing of both familiar and invented music or sound sequences in any area of the classroom or nursery, indoors or out
Making up songs in response to a range of stimuli	Spontaneous singing, often about what they are doing, while they are engaged in some activity
Making up music in response to a range of stimuli	Spontaneous music-making using instruments and sound-makers, either those specifically provided for music-making or other available resources
Making up music in response to dance	Children spontaneously play music in response to others dancing or moving in a rhythmic or expressive fashion Spontaneous movements which create sounds, e.g. using ankle or wrist bells and soundbeam
Moving in response to music	Spontaneous dance and movement
Responding to music through the use of a range of creative media, including spoken language	Spontaneous movement or vocalization in response to music
Recording musical ideas in a range of forms or media	Spontaneous mark-making to represent music
Listening to a range of live music	Opportunities to listen informally to musicians – including older children or each other
Listening to a range of recorded music	A selection of recorded music in the music area for listening through headphones

able to extend their understanding. In the same way as parents and carers engaging in protoconversations with babies pick up on and develop sounds produced by babies, experienced practitioners may be skilled at responding to and developing musical ideas initiated by children.

Conversations

In this section we first explore situations in which adults involve themselves in activities in which children are engaged. Susan Young (2000), for example, has undertaken research into musical conversations between adults and children. As part of the research, adults plan to respond to children playing tuned percussion instruments by mirroring the tunes they create and the ways in which they play the instruments. Although such activities are, in a sense, initiated by the child, the adult's decision to join in is an adult-responsive intervention and changes the nature of the activity. Had the adult not chosen to join in, the child's explorations may well have taken a different direction.

In working with young children there are many such opportunities for adult intervention. Glover (2000: 52) suggests: 'Joining in and making music alongside or in turns has direct parallels with the ways in which adults encourage children's language development by talking to them.'

In Susan Young's work, the adults interacted with individual children using a tuned percussion instrument. Glover (2000: 53) argues that 'this kind of interactive play with music should be the central mainstay of work with children in the early years' as it enables music-making to become 'a social and expressive medium alongside language'.

It is also possible to have conversations using untuned percussion instruments, or even using body rhythms, such as clapping or stamping. An adult observing a child beating a drum might decide to intervene in any of the following ways:

• echoing the rhythms played by the child on another instrument;
• varying the response, for example by playing louder or quieter, or changing the timbre by using a different beater;
• adding movements to the rhythm;
• making a tape-recording of the music.

Adults could also engage in vocal musical conversations in the same way. Playful interchanges might develop from:

• a child asking for something in a sing-song voice and the adult responding using a similar intonation;
• at the water tray, a child imitates the pattering sound as the water sprays on to a metal tray and the adult copies the sound of the child, who in turn comes back with another sound pattern;
• a child sings a line of a song and pauses, and the adult sings the next line: adult and child take turns singing the lines of the song.

When children are heard to be making up songs, or varying the words of known songs, adults may intervene to extend or maintain the child's interest by:

- asking the child to teach it to the adult;
- offering to accompany the song on an instrument such as a shaker;
- offering a new line or verse;
- developing actions or chorus response;
- recording it on a tape-recorder or writing it down;
- encouraging the child to record their song using writing, drawing or invented notation.

An adult might also see children dancing and could intervene by:

- playing an instrument to accompany the dancing;
- singing to accompany the dancing;
- joining in with the dancing.

As an alternative to joining in, adults may sometimes talk to children about their spontaneous music-making or music they are listening to. These individual interactions may sometimes develop into small group activities as other children become interested and start joining in.

Planned changes in the environment
Another way in which adults can respond to and build on children's activities is by using what they have observed to plan changes in the environment. This can lead to further child-initiated activity which will develop and extend what the child has begun. These changes would usually be introduced when children have been observed showing a sustained interest in an activity. Some examples are shown in Table 6.3.

Adults can also respond by offering informal experiences for small groups or individuals in response to their observations. These might include:

- singing informally in order to encourage children to gain confidence in singing;
- bringing in somebody, perhaps a parent, to play informally, possibly in a quiet area of the classroom, to develop children's interest in instruments;
- choosing songs or recorded music to be played informally, in response to a particular interest of a child or small group of children.

Table 6.4 gives some examples in each aspect of the music curriculum of how adults can respond to children's music-making.

Table 6.3 Planning changes to the environment after initial observation

Observation	Possible planned change to the environment
Children exploring shakers in the music area	Create a display of different shakers in the music area placing some clear plastic containers and 'fillings' such as shells, acorns, on a table near the music area
Children in the dressing-up area performing a song	Put a tape-recorder with built-in microphone into the dressing-up area
A group of children dancing	Provide a designated space with ankle or wrist bells, other instruments, ribbons, scarves and other props and perhaps recorded music
Children interested in listening to a piece of music	Place the tape-recorder in the workshop area so that children can express their response through other media such as paint, drawing or 3-dimensional work
Children playing a game about space travel	Choose a piece of electronic music to play while the children are engaged in dramatic play

Adult-directed activities

Many adults associate music with activities led by an adult. It is common practice to have a regular large-group or whole-class music session. With younger children, some of these activities might be better suited to smaller groups, in order to allow for a greater degree of interaction. As with other kinds of organized activity, staff need to ensure a balance of adult-led and child-initiated activity, with younger children needing a higher degree of opportunity for free exploration and more intimate interaction with adults and peers.

Music can also be used as a focused activity, with an adult inviting small groups of children to participate throughout the session. In this section we look at both kinds of activity.

Planned focused activities

Adults may sometimes plan organized activities in which small groups of children are asked to express their responses to a piece of music by any of the following means:

- painting, drawing or modelling while a piece of music is played to them;

Table 6.4 Adult-responsive activities in relation to each aspect of the music curriculum

Aspects of the curriculum	Adult-responsive activities: working with children
Singing	Adults join in with children's spontaneous singing in order to validate and encourage it. This might include one-to-one singing games Offering children opportunities to sing in informal situations
Playing a range of instruments and sound-making materials	Musical conversations between adults and children, where adults join in with children's spontaneous playing. This echoes the protoconversations developed between carers and babies in infancy Observations of children's sound exploration may lead adults to provide particular kinds of sound-making materials or instruments in order to stimulate further interest Offering children opportunities to join in with an adult or other experienced musician playing in informal situations
Making up songs in response to a range of stimuli	Building on observations of children's spontaneous music-making by providing tape-recorders and microphones Informal adult response to children's song-making, perhaps offering verses or developing actions or chorus response
Making up music in response to a range of stimuli	Building on observations of children's spontaneous music-making by providing tape-recorders and microphones Informal adult response to children's music-making, perhaps playing alongside with rhythms or developing musical conversations
Making up music in response to dance	Encouraging children to play instruments and other sound-makers in response to children's spontaneous movement or dance
Moving in response to music	Building on observations of children's spontaneous dance by providing space, props or music Joining in with children's spontaneous dance, either by dancing or by offering an accompaniment of some sort

Table 6.4 Continued

Aspects of the curriculum	Adult-responsive activities: working with children
Responding to music through the use of a range of creative media, including spoken language	Informal individual or small group conversations about music Providing a range of media which may promote a wider range of responses to music
Recording musical ideas in a range of forms or media	Adult records children's music-making through the use of standard or non-standard notations Adult encourages and/or supports child in recording musical ideas though invented notations
Listening to a range of live music	Choosing songs to sing informally which will develop children's musical ideas
Listening to a range of recorded music	Choosing recorded music to sing informally which will develop children's musical ideas Working with a child to make a tape-recording for the music area

- moving or dancing in response to a piece of music or percussion instruments played by adults or children;
- making 'musical maps' or graphic scores;
- making books about favourite songs, illustrated by children;
- making books or illustrations to record a musical event they have attended;
- promoting discussion of music they listen to using postcards or other small visual images.

They may also plan other music-related activities, such as:

- making shakers or other home-made instruments;
- creating a collage or books made from pictures of instruments or objects which make sounds;
- going on a listening walk and creating a tape of environmental sounds;
- close-observational drawings of musical instruments.

Whole-class or large-group sessions

Although the following activities are described as whole-class or large-group sessions, they could all be used as focused activities with small groups of children. Adults will decide on the organization appropriate to the age and experience of the children they are working with. They should also plan to ensure that all aspects of the curriculum are appropriately addressed. This type of activity may serve as an introduction or a model for children who may take the ideas offered in, for example, illustrating a story, and use them in independent activity.

- *Singing*

Sessions where children come together to sing can be used to introduce children to new songs. The repertoire might include:

- action songs;
- story songs;
- nursery rhymes;
- counting songs;
- leader–chorus songs;
- songs to which children contribute ideas;
- songs which children have made up themselves.

In addition to whole-class singing, some children may wish to perform alone or in small groups for the rest of the class.

- *Playing a range of instruments and sound-making materials*

In addition to the free exploration which children have in the music area, organized instrumental sessions can be used to broaden and develop children's playing. These activities do not require any significant degree of technical knowledge on the part of the adult leading them. Here are a few ideas:

- band sessions where children improvise music with adults or children as conductors, trying out a range of signals which must be understood by everyone involved;
- using instruments to represent moods or atmospheres depicted in a poem or picture;
- using instruments or body sounds to accompany a song;
- using instruments to illustrate or represent elements of a story;
- performance of music created by a child or group of children.

- *Making up songs and music*

Whole-group sessions can be used to offer models to children, helping them to understand the processes of songwriting, improvising and composing so that they can use them later in their own independent activities. Planned activities might include:

- making a familiar story into a song, perhaps using a familiar tune or song structure;

- making up new words to an existing tune;
- using instruments to represent moods or atmospheres depicted in a story, poem or picture;
- using instruments to illustrate or represent elements of a story;
- making up music to accompany a song or dance that some children have already created.

- *Listening to a range of live or recorded music*

The range of competence, instruments, styles and cultures demonstrated in the music chosen, whether live or recorded, should be as broad as possible. As noted earlier, although recorded music has an important part to play in children's musical development, it cannot replace live music. Planned listening activities might include:

- live performance events with invited musicians, who might include a recorder group from the primary school, members of children's families or communities, or professional performers;
- staff using their own instruments or the resources in the school to play music to children;
- getting children to listen in a whole group to short excerpts of recorded music, which might then lead to discussion, notation or other forms of response as described above;
- watching a video of a musical performance.

- *Responding to music*

Developing children's responses to music is an important precursor to the appraising that is expected of them as they go through school. More importantly, children do have strong responses to music of different types, and organized activities can help them to channel and articulate their responses. They may be encouraged to respond in a variety of ways:

- dance or movement sessions, responding to different musical starting points;
- painting, drawing or modelling in response to a musical stimulus;
- verbal responses to pieces of music, with words and phrases charted by the adult;
- improvised music representing the ideas heard in a piece of music they have listened to.

- *Recording musical ideas*

Children's music-making may be recorded using a tape-recorder. Some children may enjoy having a short tape of their own to which they can add new songs or pieces from time to time to share with others in school or at home.

In addition, children can be encouraged to find ways of writing down musical ideas. Adults do not need a knowledge of conventional music notation in order to lead this kind of activity. As discussed in Chapter 3, the aim is to help children to understand that sounds can be represented graphically.

There are many ways in which sounds or music can be written down. Giving children opportunities to invent their own notations can help children to put their ideas into a symbolic form, thus developing their thinking. At the same time it gives adults a valuable insight into children's understanding. Activities involving notation could include:

- when teaching new songs or performing known songs, drawing children's attention to the notation in songbooks. Adults do not need to understand the notation themselves in order to make children interested;
- modelling musical maps or graphic scores while listening to music, showing how different textures, timbres, speeds and pitches are represented;
- giving groups of children paper and pencil or whiteboards and markers in order to note down musical ideas while listening to a piece of music;
- suggesting that children find a way of writing down a song or music they have composed to help them remember it on a future occasion.

As in the development of literacy and numeracy, children's invented notations can play an important part in helping them to understand the function of written forms.

Integrating the three types of activity

Although it is sometimes difficult to define the boundaries between the three categories of activity outlined above, it is important that all three are included in the curriculum for the following reasons:

- child-initiated activities enable us to see what children know and can do so that we can build on our observations and plan accordingly;
- adult-directed activities enable adults to guide children's learning and to plan appropriate time and resources;
- adult-responsive activities form a bridge between the two, enabling the adult to explore the child's understanding, extend child-initiated

learning both immediately and in the longer term, and make it accessible to a wider group.

Tables 6.5 and 6.6 show how an integrated approach to the three types of activity can support learning not just for the individual but also for the wider group. In the first, an activity initiated by a child is developed into the basis for a whole-class activity which in turn stimulates further child-initiated activity. In the second, the collaborative instrumental work of two children is extended and supported by the adult's intervention to stimulate further interest in dance. In each case, a spiral of interest and development is created which the adult exploits to support progress and learning.

Assessing, recording and evaluating learning

Most early years practitioners maintain narrative, observational records of children's development across the curriculum. Practitioners always carry more information about children in their heads than they could possibly write down – the observations do, however, serve a useful purpose in that they act as a trigger for the memory, bringing to life the situation in which the child was observed. These accounts of children's day-to-day behaviour and activity need to be regularly evaluated and acted upon if they are to be of value.

Observations can be compared to the sections of the *Curriculum Guidance for the Foundation Stage* (QCA 2000) entitled 'Examples of what

Table 6.5 Example of how an integrated approach can facilitate the expansion of a child-initiated activity into a learning activity for the whole group

Child-initiated	Adult-responsive	Adult-directed
1	**2**	**3**
Child making up a song at the dough table	Adult joins in and learns the song from the child	With the child's permission, adult teaches the song to the rest of the class
4	**5**	**6**
Following this example, other children become more interested in making up their own songs	Adult writes down some of the songs with the children	Class compiles a book of their songs, with illustrations

Table 6.6 Further example of how adult intervention in child-initiated activity can support learning by the whole group

	Activity	Approach
1	Two children exploring instruments create a rhythmic pattern using drum and cymbal	Child-initiated
2	Adult takes photograph and makes a recording; displays these in music area	Adult-responsive
3	Children see the display and play the tape. They start dancing as they listen to it	Child-initiated
4	Adult joins in with the dancing and several other children become involved as well	Adult-responsive
5	Adult plans a movement session using the tape and based on the dance and also introduces new rhythmic movement patterns	Adult-directed
6	Adult changes the room around to make a bigger space where children can engage in further spontaneous movement	Adult-responsive

children do'. This in turn may lead to suggestions for planning based on the 'stepping stones' themselves.

The questions in Table 6.1 are also helpful, but only if used as an overall guide rather than a checklist. It would not be possible to maintain a meaningful record with that level of detail for every child. However, the questions can be used as a framework for reviewing observations.

Whichever of these is used, a short statement about a child's progress in all areas of experience should be noted at regular intervals, usually half-termly. Comments on creative development should include reference to children's progress in music, along with the other areas – imaginative and role play, dance and art.

As well as enabling practitioners to review children's progress, these observations can also help them to evaluate the curriculum. If, for example, observations suggest that few children are interested in the music area, practitioners should consider whether the area is sufficiently attractive or stimulating to excite the children's interest.

Involving children in evaluating their work

Duffy (1998: 133) suggests that children can be involved in the process of evaluating their creative work by exploring with them the following questions:

- What were their intentions?
- Why have they used materials or ideas in that particular way?
- Does the result satisfy them, are they happy with it?
- What would they like to do or know next?

Children may be helped to do this in music by the use of tape record-ings or video recordings. Photographs, relevant drawings or adult accounts of their songs or other musical activity in their record files might also serve as a focus for discussion between children and their key person.

Supportive parents and carers

The role of parents and carers in supporting the development of literacy and mathematics in young children is well documented. We have already seen in Chapter 5 that family support is identified as one of the preconditions for high musical achievement (Harrison and Pound 1996; Sloboda and Davidson 1996). A musical home environment can support not only the development of music but also, as we have seen, the development of communication, expressiveness and creativity.

This is recognized in schemes such as the Oxford-based Peers Early Education Partnership (PEEP) where classes are held for the parents of young children. A strong emphasis is placed on singing, rhymes and action games. Parents are given confidence in their ability to sing and helped to understand the importance of singing. Its contribution to the education of young children is valued by Sure Start, and similar schemes are being developed elsewhere in the UK.

The inequalities in home environments may affect children's musical behaviour. Children experiencing a rich musical input at home are likely to be confident when singing or exploring instruments, while children who are unused to live music-making may be less confident, reluctant to join in or even embarrassed by hearing adults in school singing or playing. Since music is so important to early childhood development these children will be disadvantaged.

In some cases, there is a rich musical life at home which is not under-stood or reflected in the school or nursery. This may be due to cultural differences or to individual preferences for particular styles of music. Children may acquire skills at home which they are unable to display in the early years setting. They may be used to a different style of singing from that which the setting offers.

Children's learning can best be supported when parents, carers and practitioners work together. The following ideas may help to promote this collaboration:

- encouraging children to sing songs that they know from home;
- encouraging parents and carers to perform for children;
- encouraging children and parents or carers to bring in recorded music from home which can be played to other children;
- encouraging parents and carers to join in music-making at school or nursery, either at designated sessions or more informally;
- making tapes of songs sung at school or nursery for children to take away and sing at home;
- making books of favourite songs so that they may be sung at home;
- inviting parents and carers in when live performances are planned, or to accompany children to live performances held elsewhere;
- asking parents and carers to recommend people who would be willing to come in and perform for children.

Supporting parents and carers

Although all parents want the best for their children, some face difficulties which mean that they themselves may need support. Goldschmied and Jackson (1994) describe work in family centres where parents of young children are offered therapeutic support in two distinct ways. In both *nurture groups* and *communication groups*, music is used to improve the relationship between parents and their children. In nurture groups, relaxation is supported by music but in addition parents are instructed to take their lead from the child, reflecting the optimum interaction which goes on between adults and neonates. There is evidence (Murray and Andrews 2000) that mothers suffering from depression find it difficult to summon up the musicality and responsiveness which is demonstrated in *motherese*. Such sessions seek to improve the bond between parents and young children.

In communication groups, sessions designed to promote collaboration in families acknowledged to have communication problems are described and the role of music in improving communication between adults and children is underlined as follows:

> Music was . . . used as a form of non-verbal communication, and parents, especially men, who were reluctant to participate in group games which they saw as childish, happily combined to produce a musical performance. The parents who took part in this group made some progress towards achieving their personal goals.
>
> (Goldschmied and Jackson 1994: 227)

Inclusion

Music is particularly helpful in enabling schools and nurseries to meet the needs of diverse groups of children. The *Curriculum Guidance for the Foundation Stage* has helpful guidance on meeting these needs and the section on creative development stresses the importance of providing opportunities for children with sensory impairment and communication difficulties, and for accommodating the needs of children with 'specific religious or cultural beliefs' (QCA 2000: 116). In this section we summarize the ways in which music can help children to be included in the life of the school or nursery. We also consider issues of access for boys and girls and for children with hearing impairment.

Cultural and linguistic diversity

- Songs can be used to support the development of English for children who are learning it as an additional language.
- Singing songs in different languages or the use of sign-supported English can introduce monolingual children to the idea of linguistic diversity.
- Social, cultural and religious diversity can be celebrated through the use of music and song.
- Familiar songs and music from their home culture can help to make children new to the UK, such as refugees and asylum seekers, feel recognized.

Learning and communication difficulties

- Music can be motivational for children with learning difficulties (Hallam 2001: 14).
- Songs are used to support children with communication difficulties, including autism, in developing the skills and vocabulary needed for conversation (Hallam 2001: 14).
- Music can be used to promote movement in children with physical disabilities.
- Music technology, such as the soundbeam, can enable children with severe and profound learning difficulties to be engaged in creative expression.
- Music supports the development of self-esteem and self-awareness in children with emotional and behavioural difficulties.
- Music can act as a calming influence on children with emotional and behavioural difficulties (Hallam 2001: 14).

Hearing impairment

Although it is the case that many deaf or hearing-impaired adults do not enjoy music, music still has a role to play in the education of deaf or hearing-impaired children. The dislike felt by some adults is often a result of their schooling. Since music can be experienced physically, it can be enjoyed by those with hearing impairments. The celebrated percussionist Evelyn Glennie may not hear music in a conventionally accepted way, but she can and does engage with it very successfully.

Those working with young children who are deaf or have hearing impairments may like to consider some of the following approaches:

- helping children with hearing impairment to feel included through the use of sign-supported English in group singing sessions;
- helping children to experience the physical impact of rhythm through movement with an adult or another child;
- allowing children to feel and observe the vibrations of instruments and other sound-makers;
- using music technology to enable children to see representations of their vocalizations or other music-making.

Although deaf or hearing-impaired babies babble in the same way as other babies, their inability to hear feedback means that this babbling may die out, and for some children it can be difficult to stimulate further vocalization. The Royal National Institute for the Blind (RNIB 1995: 115) acknowledges this difficulty in some children with multiple disabilities and offers a wide range of suggestions for encouraging vocalization, including:

- letting the child feel your mouth as you talk or sing;
- resting your lips on the child's cheek when you talk or sing;
- putting a balloon between the child's hands, resting on his or her mouth, and sing or make noises against the balloon so the child can feel the vibrations.

Gender

Although both boys and girls enjoy singing and music-making, the examples in Chapter 2 indicate that differences in the way in which they engage in music may emerge early. Boys may be attracted to drums and loud percussive instruments, while girls may show a preference for singing, dancing and quieter instruments. An illustration of this is provided by Littleton (1991, cited in Glover 2000: 49): 'When music play occurred in the house setting, girls showed a preference for movement, and boys demonstrated vocal and instrumental behaviours.'

Adults working with young children should be aware of these tendencies and the way in which they may limit children's musical development. In their interactions with children, practitioners should guard against words or actions which will reinforce stereotypes. Care should be taken to provide children with visual images and live performances which enable them to see both men and women engaged in the full range of musical activities.

Many traditional songs have words which reinforce gender stereotypes. Even when working with babies and toddlers it is important to reflect a balanced view. This can be achieved by offering variations on traditional versions which depict males and females in different roles. For example, the first verse of the song *Miss Polly had a Dolly,*

> Miss Polly had a dolly who was sick, sick, sick
> So she phoned for the doctor to come quick, quick, quick
> The doctor came with his bag and his hat
> And he knocked at the door with a rat-a-tat-tat

may be alternated with a modified version such as

> Mister Jolly had a dolly who was sick, sick, sick
> So he phoned for the doctor to come quick, quick, quick
> The doctor came with her bag and her hat
> And she knocked at the door with a rat-a-tat-tat

Alternatively, children's names (male and female) could be used instead of 'Miss Polly'.

Although to some people this may seem inconsequential, the impact of language, particularly at a young age, is very strong and can shape children's views and opinions for a long time to come.

Conclusion

The role of the adult is of fundamental importance in shaping children's learning. In relation to music, a first step for many adults may be building sufficient confidence to feel able to intervene in children's music-making or to lead adult-directed activities with a group of children. In this chapter the importance of different ways of intervening in child initiated, adult responsive and adult-directed activities has been emphasized. The role of practitioners in planning and assessing children's music-making has been outlined and we have suggested ways of encouraging the involvement of parents. Finally, the role of music in supporting inclusive practices has been considered along with issues of equality of access to music education.

Conclusion

Music is an aspect of life and an area of the curriculum which brings great pleasure to young children. They love to sing and respond to music with spontaneous movements. They show a fascination with sounds and the objects that make them. As an aspect of human development it is music that enables adults to draw children into the culture of the home and the society. It is used to attract babies' attention so that communication is made possible. It is also used to represent emotional states in a way that helps the baby to understand or to arrive at a shared meaning with care-givers. Above all, it is used by babies and carers to create situations which are characterized by fun, happiness, playfulness – all of which make learning more likely to happen.

Music is an aspect of creative development which is often taught in ways which ignore its essentially creative nature. Walker (1988: 208) comments:

> We might accept 'childish' drawings on their merit as important sources of information about children's mentality and visual representation . . . but 'childish' musical actions would be rejected as such. And it would mean that as far as musical behavior is concerned, we expect children to be like little adults; that is, we can take them seriously only when they play or compose adult music.

The fact that so little is known in the classroom about children's spontaneous songs is an indication of this lack of acceptance. Singing is an important activity but most of the singing in schools and nurseries is of songs that have been written by others. Glover (2000: 9) asks the question, 'Why are we as a community so unfamiliar with what children's music sounds like?'

Humans are born creative, and early childhood practitioners, parents and carers have a responsibility to nurture this important aspect of our make-up and to teach others to value children's own music-making.

For practitioners, the approach to music described in this book is a way of highlighting the importance of play in general, and of playfulness within music-making with young children. The long and playful childhood which humans enjoy has a biological purpose which is to ensure that we are able to respond to changes in our environment flexibly and creatively. Music has an important part to play not only as an aspect of the school curriculum but also as a foundation for the child's future.

Despite the obvious benefits of music, the subject still has a low priority for many people when developing a curriculum. Whether this is because there is a belief that only some children will benefit from it, or whether it is because practitioners themselves lack confidence, it is important to ensure that its value becomes more widely recognized. For practitioners this will mean:

- ensuring that music takes its full place in the curriculum;
- working with parents and carers to promote their awareness of the role that music can play in supporting learning;
- overcoming inhibitions about singing, dancing and making music with children.

Parents and carers also need to become aware of their own role in valuing creative musical activity as a means of communication between them and their children, and of enabling the children to express their own ideas and feelings.

Music is a powerful medium which enriches all our lives. In our lives and work with children, we need to ensure that everyone can be actively involved in making music so as to fulfil their potential as musicians. If it is music that makes us human, then in doing this we will be affirming our humanity.

Resources

Chapter 1

Songs of the type identified in this chapter can be found in:
Playsongs: Action Songs and Rhymes for Babies and Toddlers, by Sheena Roberts (available with a cassette, 1987). Playsongs Publications, 39 Byne Road, London SE26 5JF.

Chapter 2

Traditional favourites such as *Miss Polly had a Dolly*, *Walking through the Jungle* and *The Wheels on the Bus* can be found in:
This Little Puffin, compiled by Elizabeth Matterson. Harmondsworth: Penguin, 1969.
Okki Tokki Unga: Action Songs for Children, chosen by Beatrice Harrop, Linda Friend and David Gadsby. London: A&C Black, revised edition with cassette, 1994.

Details about soundbeams can be obtained from The Soundbeam Project, Unit 3, Highbury Villas, St Michael's Hill, Kingsdown, Bristol BS2 8BY. www.soundbeam.co.uk

Chapter 3

Traditional nursery rhymes can be found in:
Sing Hey Diddle Diddle: 66 Nursery Rhymes with their Traditional Tunes. London: A&C Black.

Other books containing songs mentioned in the chapter are:
Apusskidu: Songs for Children, chosen by Beatrice Harrop, Peggy Blakeley and David Gadsby. London: A&C Black, revised edition with cassette available, 1996 (includes *Train is a-coming, Ten in the Bed*).
Mango Spice: 44 Caribbean Songs, chosen by Yvonne Conolly, Gloria Cameron and Sonia Singham. London: A&C Black, 1981 (includes *Hill and Gully, Tingalayo*). *Tingalayo* can also be found in *Playsongs* (see Chapter 1).
Tongo: Rounds, Fun Songs and Starters for Younger Singers (includes *Tongo*), published by Sing for Pleasure, available from Mrs Lynda Parker, 25 Fryerning Lane, Ingatestone, Essex CM4 0DD. Tel. 01277 353691

For *The Wheels on the Bus*, see Chapter 2.

Instruments suitable for young children can be purchased from a range of suppliers, including:
Music Education Supplies Ltd, 101 Banstead Road South, Sutton, Surrey SM2 5LH. Tel. 020 8770 3866. Email: music.mes@btconnect.com

A specialist supplier of multicultural instruments is:
Knock on Wood, Granary Wharf, Leeds LS1 4BR. Tel. 0113 242 9146

For those interested in finding out more about the different approaches to music education mentioned in the text, further details can be found as follows:
The British Kodaly Academy: www.britishkodalyacademy.org.uk
The Dalcroze Society (United Kingdom), 41a Woodmansterne Road, Coulsdon, Surrey, CR5 2DJ
London Suzuki Group, 96 Farm Lane, Fulham, London SW6 1QH. Email lsg@suzukimusic.net
The Orff Society (UK), 7 Rothesay Avenue, Richmond, Surrey TW10 5EB. Email orffsocuk@talk21.com

Let's Compose: Multimedia CD-ROM for Primary Teachers, by Chris Harrison (ed.) (2001), available from Blackboard Productions, PO Box 16664, London SE23 1ZR. Tel. 020 8690 4054. www.blackboard.org.uk

Chapter 4

Readers wishing to study the claims made about the Mozart Effect by the company which markets its products can look on the website: www.mozarteffect.com

The Listening to Young Children Project is seeking to contribute an understanding of how to listen to younger children, and in particular the way creative methods and the arts are utilized by young children to articulate their understanding of the world. Further details can be obtained from Penny Lancaster, Project Director, Coram Community Campus, 49 Mecklenburgh Square, London WC1N 2QA. Tel. 020 7520 0357

The songbooks referred to in the section on communication, language and literacy are published by:
A&C Black (Publishers) Ltd
Sales & Distribution Centre:
PO Box 19, St Neots PE19 8SF
Tel. 01480 212666. Fax 01480 405014. Email: enquiries@acblackdist.co.uk
The range of songbooks and teaching materials includes *The Singing Sack, Three Singing Pigs, Three Tapping Teddies* and *Bingo Lingo*.

Soundmats or pressure pads can be purchased through a number of suppliers who stock electronic musical equipment.

There are a number of books of songs to support mathematical development, including:
Count Me In: 44 Songs and Rhymes about Numbers
Tom Thumb's Musical Maths: Developing Maths Skills with Simple Songs
both published by A&C Black (see above).

Boomwhackers are supplied by Music Education Supplies (see Chapter 3).

There was a Princess Long Ago can be found in *This Little Puffin* and *Okki Tokki Unga* (see Chapter 2).

Traditional and transparent rainsticks can be found in the catalogue of Music Education Supplies (see Chapter 3).

Chapter 5

Wind chimes can be purchased in any number of high street outlets and small specialist shops. The aim should be to collect chimes made from a variety of materials and which have different methods of construction.

For *Let's Compose*, see Chapter 3.

Further information about outdoor installations and making musical instruments from found materials can be obtained from:
Giles Leaman, Tel. 020 8802 2385
Acoustic Arts, Old Laundry, Kingswood Foundation Estate, Britannia Road, Bristol BS15 2DB. Tel 0117 935 2034. www.acousticarts.org.uk

A set of charts depicting made instruments is available from:
Pictorial Charts Educational Trust (PCET), 27 Kirchen Road, London W13 0UD. www.pcet.co.uk

Information about local scrap projects may be obtained from Waste Watch, 96 Tooley Street, London SE1 2TH. Tel. 0870 243 0136. www.wastewatch.org.uk

For information about heuristic play/treasure baskets, the seminal publication is E. Goldschmied and S. Jackson, *People Under Three* (London: Routledge, 1994). In addition, J. Manning-Morton and M. Thorp, *Key Times* (London, London Borough of Camden, 2001) have produced at-a-glance guidance on putting together treasure baskets for babies and toddlers.

An increasing range of music from around the world is available from high street music outlets. Many record companies also produce samplers or themed collections which include examples of music from different countries or traditions on a single disc. Some companies whose catalogues include a good selection of world musics are:
ARC Music, PO Box 111, East Grinstead, West Sussex, RH19 2YF. Tel. 01342 312161. www.arcmusic.co.uk
Airmail Music: www.playasound.com
Ellipsis Arts: email: elliarts@aol.com – also available through Knock On Wood (see Chapter 3)
EMI Hemisphere series: www.hemisphere-records.com
Nascente: www.nascente.co.uk
Nimbus Records Ltd: www.nimbus.ltd.uk
Putumayo World Music: www.putumayo.com
Realworld Records, Box, Corsham, Wilts SN14 9PN. http://realworld.on.net
Saydisc Records, Chipping Manor, The Chipping, Wotton-under-Edge, Glos. GL12 7AD. Tel. 01453 845036
World Music Network, 6 Abbeville Mews, 88 Clapham Park Road, London SW4 7BX. Tel. 020 7498 5252. www.worldmusic.net

Pictorial Charts Educational Trust (PCET) produce wallcharts of musical instruments from around the world (see above for contact details).

Chapter 6

The songbooks mentioned above will contain examples of the different types of songs mentioned in this chapter. Most of the more recent songbooks have accompanying cassettes or CDs.

For more information about PEEP, contact the PEEP Information Office, The PEEP Centre, Peers School, Sandy Lane West, Littlemore, Oxford OX4 6JZ. www.peep.org.uk
Resources include a short video, *Beginning with PEEP* (1998).

References

Achilles, E. (1999) Creating music environments in early childhood programs. *Young Children*, 54(1): 21–6.

Andress, B. (1991) From research to practice: preschool children and their movement responses to music. *Young Children*, 47(1): 22–7.

Athey, C. (1990) *Extending Thought in Young Children*. London: Paul Chapman.

Bamberger, J. (1982) Revisiting children's drawings of simple rhythms: function for reflection in action, in Strauss, S. (ed.) *U-Shaped Behavioural Growth*. New York: Academic Press.

Bannan, N. (2000) Instinctive singing: lifelong development of 'the child within'. *British Journal of Music Education*, 17(3): 295–301.

Bilton, H. (1998) *Outdoor Play in the Early Years: Management and Innovation*. London: David Fulton.

Blacking, J. (1976) *How Musical is Man?* London: Faber & Faber.

Blacking, J. (1987) *A Commonsense View of All Music*. Cambridge: Cambridge University Press.

Blacking, J. (1995) *Music, Culture and Experience*. London: University of Chicago Press.

Blom, E. (ed.) (1954) *Grove's Dictionary of Music and Musicians*. London: Macmillan.

Bruce, T. (1987) *Early Childhood Education*. London: Hodder & Stoughton.

Bruner, J. (1982) What is representation?, in Roberts, M. and Tamburrini, J. (eds) *Child Development 0–5*. Edinburgh: Holmes McDougall.

Campbell, P.S. (1998) *Songs in their Heads*. New York: Oxford University Press.

Carr, M. (2001) *Assessment in Early Childhood – Learning Stories*. London: Paul Chapman.

Carter, H. (1998) *Mapping the Mind*. London: Phoenix.

Chatwin, B. (1987) *Songlines*. London: Picador/Pan Books.

Clark, M. (1976) *Young Fluent Readers*. London: Heinemann.

Dale, T. (1995) Musical play structures. *Primary Music Today*, 1: 20–1.

Davidson, L. (1994) Songsinging by young and old: a developmental approach to music, in Aiello, R. (ed.) *Musical Preceptions*. New York: Oxford University Press.

Davidson, L. and Scripp, L. (1986) Young children's musical representations: windows on musical cognition, in Sloboda, J. (ed.) *Generative Processes in Music*. New York: Oxford University Press.

Davies, C. (1992) Listen to my song: a study of songs invented by children aged 5 to 7 years. *British Journal of Music Education*, 9: 19–48.

Davies, C. (1994) I can't teach music – so we just sing, in Aubrey, C. (ed.) *The Role of Subject Knowledge in the Early Years of Schooling*. London: Falmer Press.

Davies, C. (1997) Song lines. *Music Teacher*, 76(7): 15–19.

Devereux, P. (2001) *Stone Age Soundtracks*. London: Channel 4 Publications.

Donnachie, I. (2000) *Robert Owen: Owen of New Lanark and New Harmony*. East Linton: Tuckwell Press.

Douglas, S. and Willatts, P. (1994) The relationship between musical ability and literacy skills. *Journal of Research in Reading*, 17(2): 99–107.

Dowling, M. (2000) *Young Children's Personal, Social and Emotional Development*. London: Paul Chapman.

Duffy, B. (1998) *Supporting Creativity and Imagination in the Early Years*. Buckingham: Open University Press.

Dunn, J. (1998) *The Beginnings of Social Understanding*. Cambridge, MA: Harvard University Press.

Duran, L. (1999) Mali/Guinea – Mande sounds: West Africa's musical powerhouse, in Broughton, S., Ellingham, M. and Trillo, R. (eds) *World Music: The Rough Guide*, Vol. 1. London: Rough Guides.

Durkin, K. and Townsend, J. (1997) Research note: influence of linguistic factors on young school children's responses to musical pitch tests – a preliminary test. *Psychology of Music*, 25: 186–91.

Dyson, A. (2001) Where are the childhoods in childhood literacy? An exploration in outer (school) space. *Journal of Early Childhood Literacy*, 1(1): 9–39.

East, H. (1998) *The Singing Sack: 28 Song Stories from Around the World*. London: A&C Black.

Edwards, C., Gandini, I. and Forman, G. (1993) *The Hundred Languages of Children*. Norwood, NJ: Ablex.

Egan, K. (1991) *Primary Understanding*. London: Routledge.

Eliot, L. (1999) *Early Intelligence*. London: Penguin.

Exley, H. (1991) *Music Lovers' Quotations*. Watford: Exley.

Fernald, A. (1992) Human maternal vocalisations to infants as biologically relevant signals: an evolutionary perspective, in Barkow, J.H., Cosmides, L. and Tooby, J. (eds) *The Adapted Mind: Evolutionary Psychology and the Generalisation of Culture*. Oxford: Oxford University Press.

Fisher, J. (1998) *Starting with the Child?* Buckingham: Open University Press.

Gardner, H. (1993a) *Frames of Mind*, 2nd edn. London: Harper Collins.

Gardner, H. (1993b) *The Unschooled Mind*. London: Fontana.

Gardner, H. (1994) *The Arts and Human Development*. New York: Basic Books.

Gardner, H. (1999) *Intelligence Reframed*. New York: Basic Books.

Glover, J. (2000) *Children Composing 4–14*. London: Routledge/Falmer.

Goldschmied, E. and Jackson, S. (1994) *People Under Three*. London: Routledge.

Goleman, D. (1996) *Emotional Intelligence*. London: Fontana.

Goswami, U. and Bryant, P. (1990) *Phonological Skills and Learning to Read*. London: Lawrence Erlbaum Associates.

Gregory, A.H. (1997) The roles of music in society: the ethnomusicological perspective, in Hargreaves, D.J. and North, A.C. (eds) *The Social Psychology of Music*. Oxford: Oxford University Press.

Gura, P. (ed.) (1992) *Exploring Learning: Young Children and Blockplay*. London: Paul Chapman.

Hallam, S. (2001) *The Power of Music*. London: Performing Rights Society.

Hargreaves, D. and Galton, M. (1992) Aesthetic learning: psychological theory and educational practice, in Reimer, B. and Smith, R. (eds) *NSSE Yearbook on the Arts in Education*. Chicago: NSSE.

Harris, P. (2000) *The Work of the Imagination*. Oxford: Blackwell.

Harrison, C. (2001*) Let's Compose – A Guide for Teachers at Key Stages 1 and 2*. London: Blackboard Productions (CD-ROM).

Harrison, C. and Pound, L. (1992) *Talking Music: A New Approach to Music in the National Curriculum at Key Stages 1 and 2*. London: Greenwich Professional Development Centre.

Harrison, C. and Pound, L. (1996) Talking Music: Empowering Children as Musical Communicators. *British Journal of Music Education*, 13(3): 233–42.

Hildebrandt, C. (1998) Creativity in music and early childhood. *Young Children*, 53(6): 68–74.

HMI (Her Majesty's Inspectorate of Schools) (1985) *Music from 5 to 16*. London: HMSO.

Holdaway, D. (1979) *The Foundations of Literacy*. Gosford, NSW: Ashton Scholastic.

Holdaway, D. (1980) *Independence in Reading*. Gosford, NSW: Ashton Scholastic.

Karmiloff-Smith, A. (1994) *Baby It's You!* London: Ebury Press.

Kendall, S. (1986) The harmony of human life: an exploration of the ideas of Pestalozzi and Froebel in relation to music education. *British Journal of Music Education*, 3(1): 35–48.

Kratus, J. (1994) Relationships among children's music audiation and their compositional processes and products. *Journal of Research in Music Education*, 42(2): 115–30.

LeDoux, J. (1999) *The Emotional Brain*. London: Weidenfeld & Nicolson.

Lundin, A. and Sandberg, A. (2001) The music in Swedish preschools. *British Journal of Music Education*, 18(3): 241–50.

MacGregor, H. (1999) *Bingo Lingo*. London: A&C Black.

Maclean, M., Bryant, P. and Bradley, L. (1987) Rhymes, nursery rhymes, and reading in early childhood. *Merrill–Palmer Quarterly*, 33(3): 255–81.

Manning-Morton, J. and Thorp, M. (2001) *Key Times*. London, London Borough of Camden.

Matthews, J. (1994) *Helping Children to Draw and Paint in Early Childhood*. London: Hodder & Stoughton.

Merriam, A. (1964) *The Anthropology of Music*. Northwestern University Press.

Mihill, C. (1993) The myth of the 'gifted' musician. *The Guardian*, 1 September.

Montague-Smith, A. (1997) *Mathematics in Nursery Education*. London: David Fulton.

Moog, H. (1976) *The Musical Experience of the Pre-school Child*, trans. C. Clarke. London: Schott.

Murray, L. and Andrews, L. (2000) *The Social Baby*. Richmond: C.P. Publishing.

NACCCE (1999) *All Our Futures: Creativity, Culture and Education*. Sudbury: DfEE Publications.

Odam, G. (1995) *The Sounding Symbol*. Cheltenham: Stanley Thornes.

Ouvry, M. (in press) *Sounds Like Playing*. London: National Early Years Network.

Papousek, H. (1994) To the evolution of human musicality and musical education, in Deliege, I. (ed.) *Proceedings of the 3rd International Conference on Music Perception and Cognition*. Liege: ESCOM.

Papousek, H. and Papousek, M. (1994) Early musicality and caregivers' infant-directed speech, in Deliege, I. (ed.) *Proceedings of the 3rd International Conference for Music Perception and Cognition*. Liege: ESCOM.

Post, J. and Hohmann, M. (2000) *Tender Care and Early Learning*. Ypsilanti, MI: High/Scope Press.

Pound, L. (2001) *Cultural Contexts and Young Children's Personal, Social and Emotional Development*. London: University of North London.

Pound, L. (2002) Breadth and depth in early foundations, in Fisher, J. (ed.) *The Foundations of Learning*. Buckingham: Open University Press.

Powell, A. (2001) Orchestral manoeuvres in the park. *The Guardian Weekend*, 3 March.

Pugh, A. and Pugh, L. (1998) *Music in the Early Years*. London: Routledge.

QCA (1999) *The National Curriculum for England: Music*. London: DfEE/QCA.

QCA (2000) *Curriculum Guidance for the Foundation Stage*. London: DfEE/QCA.

QCA (2001a) *Guidance for Teaching Gifted and Talented Pupils*. www.nc.uk.net/gt (accessed 20 November 2001).

QCA (2001b) *Planning for Learning in the Foundation Stage*. London: DfES/QCA.

Ramachandran, V.S. and Blakeslee, S. (1999) *Phantoms in the Brain*. London: Fourth Estate.

Revesz, G. (1954) *Introduction to the Psychology of Music*. Norman, OK: University of Oklahoma Press.

RNIB (Royal National Institute for the Blind) (1995) *Play It My Way*. London: HMSO.

Shuter-Dyson, R. and Gabriel, C. (1981) *The Psychology of Musical Ability*. London: Methuen.

Siegel, D. (1999) *The Developing Mind*. New York: Guilford Press.

Sloboda, J. (1985) *The Musical Mind*. Oxford: Oxford University Press.

Sloboda, J. (1994) Music performance: expression and the development of excellence, in Aiello, R. with Sloboda, J. (eds) *Musical Perceptions*. Oxford: Oxford University Press.

Sloboda, J. and Davidson, J. (1996) The young performing musician, in Deliege, I. and Sloboda, J. (eds) *Musical Beginnings*. Oxford: Oxford University Press.

Small, C. (1998) *Musicking*. Hanover, NH: University Press of New England.

Smallberry Green Primary School, Isleworth (1997) Outdoor musical play area. *Primary Music Today*, 9: 23–7.

Smidt, S. (1998) *A Guide to Early Years Practice*. London: Routledge.

Smith, D. (2001) A paradox of musical pitch, *Monitor on Psychology*, 32(7). http://www.apa.org/monitor/julaug01/musicpitch.html

Smith, P.K. and Cowie, H. (1988) *Understanding Children's Development*. Oxford: Basil Blackwell.

Sosniak, L.A. (1985). Learning to be a concert pianist, in Bloom, B. (ed.) *Developing Talent in Young People*. New York: Ballantine.

Stead, P. (1999) Music, in Bigger, S. and Brown, E. *Spiritual, Moral, Social and Cultural Education*. London: David Fulton.

Storr, A. (1992) *Music and the Mind*. London: Harper & Collins.

Sundin, B. (1997) Musical creativity in childhood – a research project in retrospect. *Research Studies in Music Education*, 9: 48–57.

Suthers, L. (1993) Introducing young children to live orchestral performance. *Early Child Development and Care*, 90: 55–64.

Swanwick, K. (1988) *Music, Mind and Education*. London: Routledge.

Swanwick, K. and Tillman, J. (1986) The sequence of musical development. *British Journal of Music Education*, 3(3): 305–39.

Temple, C., Nathan, R., Burris, N. and Temple, F. (1988) *The Beginnings of Writing*, 2nd edn. Newton, MA: Allyn & Bacon.

Tomas, L. and Gil, V. (2000) *Teddy's Train*. Oxford: Oxford University Press.

Trehub, S., Schellenberg, E. and Hill, D. (1997) The origins of music perception and cognition: a developmental perspective, in Deliege, I. and Sloboda, J. (eds) *Perception and Cognition of Music*. Hove: Psychology Press.

Trevarthen, C. (1979) Communication and co-operation in early infancy: a description of primary intersubjectivity, in Bullowa, M. (ed.) *Before Speech: The Beginnings of Human Communication*. London: Cambridge University Press.

Trevarthen, C. (1987) Sharing makes sense: intersubjectivity and the making of an infant's meaning, in Steele, R. and Treadgold, T. (eds) *Essays in Honour of Michael Halliday*. Amsterdam/Philadelphia: John Benjamins.

Trevarthen, C. (1989) Signs before speech, in Sebeok, T.A. and Umiker-Sebeok, J. (eds) *The Semiotic Web*. Berlin: Mouton de Gruyter.

Trevarthen, C. (1998) The child's need to learn a culture, in Woodhead, M., Faulkner, D. and Littleton, K. (eds) *Cultural Worlds of Early Childhood*. London: Routledge/The Open University.

Trevarthen, C. and Marwick, H. (1986) Signs of motivation for speech in infants, and the nature of a mother's support for development of language, in Lindblom, B. and Zetterstrom, R. (eds) *Precursors of Early Speech*. Basingstoke: Macmillan.

Tyrrell, J. (2001) *The Power of Fantasy in Early Learning: A Connective Pedagogy*. London: Routledge.

Umansky, K. (1994) *Three Singing Pigs*. London: A&C Black.

Umansky, K. (2000) *Three Tapping Teddies*. London, A&C Black.

Upitis, R. (1990) *This Too Is Music*. Portsmouth, NH: Heinemann.

Upitis, R. (1992) Technology and music: an intertwining dance. *Computers Education*, 18(1–3): 243–50.

Wales, R. (1990) Children's pictures, in Grieve, R. and Hughes, M. (eds) *Understanding Children*. Oxford: Blackwell.

Walker, R. (1988) In search of a child's musical imagination, in Egan, K. and Nadaner, D. (eds) *Imagination and Education*. Milton Keynes: Open University Press.

Weir, R. (1962) *Language in the Crib*. The Hague: Mouton.

Welch, G. (1998) Early childhood musical development. *Research Studies in Music Education*, 11: 27–41.

Wells, G. and Nicholls, J. (eds) (1985) *Language and Learning: An Interactional Perspective*. Lewes: Falmer Press.

Wright, J. (1996) Rhyme and reading. *Primary Music Today*, 6: 13–14.

Young, S. (2000) Spontaneous music-making on instruments in the nursery: reporting a research project and some implications for practice. Paper presented at the British Educational Research Association Annual Conference, Cardiff University, 7–9 September.

Young, S. and Glover, J. (1998) *Music in the Early Years*. London: Falmer Press.

Index

THE FOUNDATIONS OF LEARNING

Julie Fisher (ed.)

The introduction of the Foundation Stage for children age 3 to becoming 6, has had a profound impact on policy and practice in early education in the UK. The choice of the word 'foundation' to describe this first stage of learning has emphasized the importance of children's earliest experiences in underpinning all their subsequent attitudes and achievements. In this innovative and challenging book, Julie Fisher has brought together some of the country's leading early years specialists to explore how educators can establish firm foundations for young children's learning. The themes in the book are stimulated by the metaphor of 'foundations', with an introduction by an architect who explains the principles of establishing firm foundations for buildings. Each of these established engineering principles is then creatively explored from an educational perspective as the authors seek to question how the foundations laid for buildings can offer fresh insights into the principles for creating firm foundations for learning.

Contents
Introduction: the importance of firm foundations . . . an analogy with architecture –
Breadth and depth in early foundations – High levels of achievement for young
children – The impact of stress on early development – Meeting the needs of disadvan-
taged children – Making meaningful connections in early learning – Assessing what
matters in the early years – The consequences of inadequate investment in the early
years – Conclusions: the foundations of learning – References – Index.

Contributors
Tony Bertram, Adrian Cooper, Marion Dowling, Margaret Edgington, Julie Fisher, Christine Pascal, Linda Pound, Gillian Pugh OBE, Wendy Scott, Pauline Trudell.

158pp   0 335 20991 2 (Paperback)   0 335 20992 0 (Hardback)

DOING EARLY CHILDHOOD RESEARCH
INTERNATIONAL PERSPECTIVES ON THEORY AND PRACTICE

Glenda Mac Naughton, Sharne A. Rolfe and Iram Siraj-Blatchford

Doing Early Childhood Research demystifies the research process. An international team of experienced researchers shows how to select the right questions and use the appropriate methods to investigate important issues in early childhood.

The editors and authors provide a thorough introduction to the most common research methods used in the early childhood context. Reflecting the multidisciplinary nature of much early childhood research, they cover a wide range of conventional and newer approaches including observation, small surveys, action research, ethnography, policy analysis and poststructuralist approaches.

They explain clearly how to set up research projects which are theoretically grounded, well-designed, rigorously analysed, feasible and ethically fair. Each chapter is illustrated with examples and case studies.

Doing Early Childhood Research is essential reading for new researchers and students inexperienced in conducting research.

Contents
Introduction – Part I: The nature of research – Research as a tool – The research process – Paradigms, methods and knowledge – Doing research for the first time – Ethics in early childhood research – Part II: Analysis and design – Design issues – Quantitative designs and statistical analysis – Qualitative designs and analysis – Equity issues in research design – Part III: The research process in action – Surveys and questionnaires: an evaluative case study – Interviewing children – Interviewing adults – An ethnographic approach to researching young children's learning – Action research – Direct observation – Policy research – Developing reciprocity in a multi-method small-scale research study – Appendix: Getting the terms right – Glossary – References – Index.

Contributors
Liz Brooker, Sheralyn Campbell, Leslie Cannold, Margaret M. Coady, Anne Edwards, Ann Farrell, Susan Grieshaber, Linda Harrison, Alan Hayes, Patrick Hughes, Glenda Mac Naughton, Mindy Blaise Ochsner, Sharne A. Rolfe, Sharon Ryan, Iram Siraj-Blatchford, John Siraj-Blatchford.

320pp   0 335 20902 5 (Paperback)

EXPERIENCING REGGIO EMILIA
IMPLICATIONS FOR PRE-SCHOOL PROVISION

Lesley Abbott and Cathy Nutbrown (eds.)

Early education, internationally, is the focus of much challenge and debate. Various approaches to teaching young children are being developed and advocated, but the focus is often on curriculum content with the processes of learning as a secondary issue. The most important consideration in early education is the way in which young children learn. Their transferable skills of communication, collaboration and investigation can underpin all aspects of learning. These elements form the main focus of work in a group of pre-schools in an area of Northern Italy that has earned an international reputation for innovative practice and pedagogy.

The experience of Reggio Emilia, in providing challenges to accepted approaches to early childhood education in many countries, is widely acknowledged. Since 1963, when the Italian municipality of Reggio Emilia began setting up its network of educational services for 0- to 6-year-olds, the 'Reggio approach' has gained worldwide recognition. Numerous visitors have been impressed by the acknowledgement given to the potential of children, the organization and quality of the environments created, the promotion of collegiality and the climate of co-participation of families in the educational project.

This book reflects the impressions and experiences of the Reggio Emilia approach gained by a range of early childhood educators following a study visit to the region. It focusses on key issues such as staffing, training, working with parents, play, learning, the culture of early childhood and special educational needs, from a variety of perspectives, and will provide a welcome challenge to thinking for both practitioners and policy makers.

Contents
Experiencing Reggio Emilia – Perceptions of play – a question of priorities? – Listening and learning – Quality and the role of the pedagogista *Sunniva's extra pocket: a parent's reflections – Sam's invisible extra gear: a parent's view – Special needs or special rights? – A question of inclusion – Creating places for living and learning – 'She's back!' The impact of my visit to Reggio Emilia on a group of 3- and 4-year-olds – Journeying above the 'sea of fog': reflections on personal professional development inspired by Reggio – A journey into reality – Creating a palette of opportunities: situations for learning in the early years – The otherness of Reggio – Questions and challenges: continuing the dialogue – Glossary – Index.*

Contributors
Lesley Abbott, John Bishop, Robin Duckett, Kath Hirst, Caroline Hunter, Cynthia Knight, Jenny Leask, Peter Moss, Angela Nurse, Cathy Nutbrown, Christine Parker, Sylvia Philips, Wendy Scott

176pp   0 335 20703 0 (Paperback)   0 335 20704 9 (Hardback)